MacBook
SENIORS GUIDE

*A complete, Easy-to-Follow Manual to Master Your New Device.
Discover All Features with **Illustrated Step-by-Step Instructions &
Helpful Tips** to Maximize Your MacBook Experience*

- ✓ Settings
- ✓ Security
- ✓ Entertainment
- ✓ Essential Apps
- ✓ macOS Sonoma
- ✓ Tips & Tricks
- ✓ Communications

VIN MAYER

Table of Contents

INTRODUCTION TO MACBOOK GUIDE

A MacBook is a line of laptop computers designed and manufactured by Apple Inc. They are known for their sleek design, high-quality build, and seamless integration with the macOS operating system. This guide aims to provide you with a comprehensive introduction to MacBook, covering its history, hardware, software, and essential features.

Hardware Components:

- **Display:** MacBooks come in various screen sizes, with Retina displays offering high-resolution visuals.
- **Processor:** MacBooks are equipped with Intel or Apple-designed M-series processors, providing excellent performance and energy efficiency.
- **Storage:** They feature fast solid-state drives (SSDs) for storage, which significantly improve speed and responsiveness.
- **RAM:** MacBooks come with varying amounts of RAM (memory), with options to upgrade in some models.
- **Battery:** Apple prides itself on long battery life, allowing users to work on the go without constant charging.
- **Ports:** Ports may vary among models, with some featuring USB-C/Thunderbolt ports, headphone jacks, and more.

MacOS Operating System:

- MacBooks run on macOS, Apple's desktop operating system.
- macOS offers a user-friendly interface, security features, and seamless integration with other Apple devices.
- Regular updates provide new features and security enhancements.

Essential Features:

Trackpad and Keyboard: MacBooks have precision trackpads and keyboards designed for comfortable typing and navigation.

Touch Bar (on some models): A customizable touch-sensitive bar that offers context-specific controls.

- **FaceTime and iSight Camera:** Built-in cameras for video conferencing and photography.
- **Siri:** Apple's virtual assistant is integrated into macOS for voice commands and assistance.
- **File Management:** The Finder app helps manage files and documents efficiently.
- **App Store:** Access a wide range of applications for productivity, creativity, and entertainment.
- **iCloud Integration:** Seamlessly sync and backup data across Apple devices.
- **Security:** MacBooks are known for their robust security features, including Gatekeeper and FileVault.
- **Accessibility:** A suite of accessibility features to assist users with disabilities.
- **Software Updates:** macOS receives regular updates with bug fixes and new features.

Tips for New MacBook Users:

- Set up iCloud for easy data syncing.
- Familiarize yourself with keyboard shortcuts and trackpad gestures for efficient navigation.
- Customize your MacBook's settings to suit your preferences.
- Explore the Mac App Store to find useful applications.
- Regularly update your macOS for security and performance improvements.

In conclusion, a MacBook is a powerful and elegant laptop designed to offer a premium computing experience. With its hardware, macOS, and essential features, it provides a versatile platform for productivity, creativity, and entertainment. Whether you're a professional, student, or casual user, a MacBook can meet a wide range of computing needs.

BRIEF HISTORY AND EVOLUTION OF THE MACBOOK

The MacBook is a line of laptop computers designed and manufactured by Apple Inc. It has a rich history of innovation and evolution since its introduction. Let's explore its journey from the early days to the present:

Early Days (2006):
- The first MacBook was introduced on May 16, 2006, replacing the iBook and PowerBook lines.
- It featured a 13.3-inch display and was available in both white and black plastic casings.
- The MacBook ran on Intel processors, marking Apple's transition from PowerPC chips.

Transition to Aluminum Unibody (2008):
- In 2008, Apple introduced the MacBook Air, a super-thin and lightweight model that set a new standard for ultrabooks.
- The MacBook line also underwent a significant design change, adopting a unibody aluminum construction for improved durability and aesthetics.
- The MacBook Pro received updates with faster processors and better graphics.

Retina Displays (2012):
- In 2012, Apple introduced the first MacBook Pro with a Retina display, offering a stunning high-resolution screen.
- This marked a shift towards higher-quality displays across the MacBook lineup.
- The MacBook Air was updated with improved battery life and performance.

MacBook Air Reinvention (2018):
- In 2018, Apple reinvented the MacBook Air, making it thinner, lighter, and more powerful.
- The MacBook Air also adopted the Retina display, providing crisp visuals.
- The butterfly keyboard was introduced but faced criticism for reliability issues.

Apple Silicon Transition (2020):
- In November 2020, Apple announced its transition from Intel processors to custom-designed Apple Silicon, starting with the M1 chip.
- The M1 MacBook Air and MacBook Pro were released, showcasing impressive performance and energy efficiency.
- This marked a significant shift in the Mac ecosystem's architecture.

Ongoing Innovation (2021 - Present):
- Apple continued to release updated MacBook models, both Intel-based and Apple Silicon-based, offering various configurations to cater to different user needs.
- The butterfly keyboard was phased out in favor of the improved Magic Keyboard.
- Displays have seen improvements in color accuracy, brightness, and ProMotion technology.

macOS Updates:
- Over the years, MacBooks have been powered by various macOS versions, each bringing new features, security enhancements, and user interface improvements.
- macOS has evolved to seamlessly integrate with other Apple devices through features like Continuity, Handoff, and iCloud.

Sustainability Initiatives:
- Apple has placed a strong emphasis on environmental sustainability, using recycled materials in MacBook manufacturing and promoting trade-in and recycling programs.

The MacBook has evolved from its humble beginnings as a plastic laptop to a premium line of computers known for their sleek design, high-quality build, and integration with Apple's ecosystem. With each iteration, Apple has pushed the boundaries of technology and design, making the MacBook a symbol of innovation in the laptop industry.

IMPORTANCE AND POPULARITY OF MACBOOKS

MacBooks, Apple's line of laptops, hold significant importance and enjoy widespread popularity for a variety of reasons. Below, we'll delve into the key factors that contribute to their importance and popularity:

Build Quality and Design:
- Apple's meticulous attention to design and build quality is a hallmark of MacBooks. Their premium aluminum unibody construction not only looks sleek but also offers exceptional durability.

- The attention to detail extends to the keyboard, trackpad, and display, ensuring a top-notch user experience.

Operating System (macOS):
- MacBooks run on macOS, Apple's proprietary operating system known for its user-friendly interface, robust security features, and seamless integration with other Apple devices.
- macOS receives regular updates, providing users with new features, performance improvements, and enhanced security.

Performance and Efficiency:
- MacBooks are equipped with powerful processors, including Apple's custom-designed M-series chips, offering excellent performance for a wide range of tasks.
- The integration of SSD storage results in quick boot times and snappy application performance.
- Efficient power management ensures long battery life, making MacBooks ideal for on-the-go users.

Display Quality:
- Many MacBook models feature Retina displays with high resolution, wide color gamuts, and excellent brightness. This makes them suitable for creative professionals, multimedia consumption, and productivity tasks.
- Features like True Tone and ProMotion technology further enhance the viewing experience.

Ecosystem Integration:
- MacBooks seamlessly integrate with other Apple devices through features like iCloud, Continuity, and Handoff. This allows users to switch between devices effortlessly and share content seamlessly.

Software Ecosystem:
- Mac App Store, where users can find productivity tools, creative software, and entertainment apps.
- MacBooks can also run Windows through Boot Camp or virtualization software, expanding their software compatibility.

Security and Privacy:
- The macOS ecosystem offers a wide range of applications and software, including the
- Apple places a strong emphasis on user security and privacy. Features like Gatekeeper, FileVault, and Touch ID (or Face ID) enhance device security.
- Regular security updates keep MacBooks protected against emerging threats.

Customer Support and Service:
- Apple's customer support and service are highly regarded. Users have access to AppleCare for extended support, and Apple's retail stores and authorized service providers offer convenient repair and maintenance options.

Creative and Professional Tools:
- MacBooks are favored by creative professionals for their performance in graphics-intensive applications. Software like Final Cut Pro X and Logic Pro X is optimized for macOS, making MacBooks the preferred choice for video editing, music production, and graphic design.

Sustainability Initiatives:
- Apple has made significant strides in environmental sustainability, and many users appreciate the company's commitment to reducing its carbon footprint, using recycled materials, and promoting recycling programs.

Brand Loyalty and Community:
- Apple has a dedicated and passionate user community, and many users feel a strong sense of brand loyalty.
- The MacBook's popularity is bolstered by word-of-mouth recommendations and a loyal customer base.

In summary, the importance and popularity of MacBooks can be attributed to their exceptional build quality, high-performance hardware, user-friendly software, ecosystem integration, strong security measures, and the overall Apple brand experience. These factors have cemented MacBooks as a preferred choice for a wide range of users, from students and creative professionals to business executives and everyday consumers.

1. UNDERSTANDING MACBOOK MODELS

Apple offers a diverse range of MacBook models to cater to various user needs, from casual consumers to professional creatives and developers.

Understanding these models involves considering their key features, capabilities, and target audiences. As of my last knowledge update in September 2021, here's a comprehensive overview of the major MacBook models:

MacBook Air:

- **Target Audience:** General consumers, students, and travelers.

Key Features:
- Ultra-thin and lightweight design, making it highly portable.
- Retina display for sharp visuals.
- Long battery life for all-day use.
- Typically features fanless, energy-efficient processors for silent operation.
- Good balance of performance and portability.
- Excellent for web browsing, media consumption, and everyday tasks.
- Integrated Magic Keyboard and trackpad.
- Limited number of ports (USB-C/Thunderbolt).

MacBook Pro (13-inch):

- **Target Audience:** Professionals, students, and creatives seeking a balance between power and portability.

Key Features:
- Retina display with high resolution.
- More powerful processors compared to the MacBook Air.
- Suitable for tasks like video editing, software development, and graphic design.
- Robust build quality.
- Magic Keyboard.
- Various configurations available, including Intel and Apple Silicon (M1) models.
- A moderate number of ports, including Thunderbolt 3 (USB-C).

MacBook Pro (16-inch):

Target Audience: Professional users requiring high performance and a larger display.

Key Features:
- Larger Retina display for enhanced productivity and content creation.
- Powerful processors, including Intel and Apple Silicon (M1 Pro and M1 Max).
- Ideal for demanding tasks such as 3D rendering, video production, and professional-grade software.
- Excellent audio quality with enhanced speakers.
- Larger chassis with more ports, including USB-C/Thunderbolt and traditional HDMI and MagSafe.
- Premium build quality and advanced thermal management.

MacBook (12-inch) [Discontinued]:

- **Target Audience:** Users who prioritize extreme portability.

Key Features:
- Ultra-slim and lightweight design.
- Retina display.
- Fanless design with low-power Intel processors.
- Single USB-C port for charging and connectivity.
- Limited processing power, suitable for basic tasks.

MacBook Air with Apple Silicon (M1):
- **Target Audience:** General consumers, students, and travelers.

Key Features:
- Similar to the Intel-based MacBook Air but powered by Apple's custom-designed M1 chip.
- Offers significant performance and efficiency improvements.
- Enhanced graphics and battery life.
- Runs both native M1 and Intel apps through Rosetta 2 translation.
- Retains the slim and lightweight design.

MacBook Pro with Apple Silicon (M1):
- **Target Audience:** Professionals and power users.

Key Features:
- Utilizes Apple's M1 chip for exceptional performance and energy efficiency.
- Significant gains in CPU and GPU performance.
- Excellent for tasks like video editing, software development, and more.
- Features the Magic Keyboard.
- Supports running both M1 and Intel apps through Rosetta 2.
- Limited port options (USB-C/Thunderbolt).

Please note that Apple frequently updates its product lineup, so there may have been new releases and changes in MacBook models since my last knowledge update in September 2021. When considering a MacBook, it's important to assess your specific needs and budget, as well as the latest available models and configurations to make an informed choice that aligns with your requirements.

MACBOOK AIR VS. MACBOOK PRO: A DETAILED COMPARISON

The choice between a MacBook Air and a MacBook Pro depends on your specific needs and priorities. To help you make an informed decision, let's compare these two popular MacBook models in various aspects:

Performance:
- **Book Air:** MacThe MacBook Air is designed for everyday computing tasks. It typically features energy-efficient processors, such as Intel's Core i3, i5, or i7 (before the introduction of Apple Silicon M1). While it offers good performance for web browsing, document editing, and media consumption, it may struggle with heavy multitasking or resource-intensive applications.
- **MacBook Pro:** The MacBook Pro is available in both 13-inch and 16-inch models, with more powerful processors, including Intel's Core i5, i7, and i9 (in Intel-based models) or Apple's custom-designed M1, M1 Pro, and M1 Max chips (in Apple Silicon models). MacBook Pro models offer significantly higher processing power, making them suitable for demanding tasks like video editing, 3D rendering, and software development.

Display:
- **MacBook Air:** The MacBook Air features a Retina display with good color accuracy and resolution. It's suitable for general media consumption, document work, and casual photo editing.
- **MacBook Pro:** MacBook Pro models come with Retina displays as well, but they tend to be brighter and offer better color accuracy. The 16-inch MacBook Pro, in particular, is ideal for professional tasks that require precise color representation.

Portability:
- **MacBook Air:** The MacBook Air is known for its ultra-portable design. It's thin, lightweight, and easy to carry, making it an excellent choice for travelers and students.
- **MacBook Pro:** While the 13-inch MacBook Pro is also quite portable, the 16-inch model is larger and heavier. It's better suited for those who need a balance between performance and portability but aren't concerned about the absolute lightest and thinnest design.

Battery Life:

- **MacBook Air:** The MacBook Air boasts excellent battery life. It can last all day on a single charge, making it great for users who need a laptop for extended periods away from a power source.
- **MacBook Pro:** The battery life of the MacBook Pro models varies. The 13-inch MacBook Pro has good battery life but may not match the Air. The 16-inch MacBook Pro, due to its more powerful components, may require more frequent charging during intensive tasks.

Graphics:
- **MacBook Air:** The MacBook Air traditionally had integrated graphics. However, the Apple Silicon M1 chip in newer models significantly improves graphics performance, making it suitable for light to moderate graphics tasks.
- **MacBook Pro:** MacBook Pro models, especially the 16-inch version and those with discrete GPUs (in Intel-based models), offer superior graphics performance. They are better suited for graphics-intensive tasks like video editing and 3D rendering.

Price:
- **MacBook Air:** The MacBook Air is generally more affordable than MacBook Pro models, making it an attractive option for budget-conscious users.
- **MacBook Pro:** MacBook Pro models tend to be more expensive due to their higher performance and professional-grade features.

Keyboard:

- **MacBook Air:** The MacBook Air features the Magic Keyboard, known for its comfortable and reliable typing experience.
- **MacBook Pro:** All recent MacBook Pro models also come with the Magic Keyboard, replacing the controversial butterfly keyboard of earlier models.

Ports:
- **MacBook Air:** The MacBook Air has a limited number of ports, typically only USB-C/Thunderbolt 3 ports and a headphone jack.
- **MacBook Pro:** MacBook Pro models offer more ports, including USB-C/Thunderbolt, HDMI (in some models), and additional Thunderbolt ports (in the 16-inch model).

Fan and Cooling:
- **MacBook Air:** The MacBook Air is fanless (in Intel models) or has a quiet fan (in Apple Silicon models), offering silent operation.
- **MacBook Pro:** MacBook Pro models, especially the 16-inch version, have robust cooling systems to manage heat during demanding tasks, which can result in fan noise.

Use Cases:

- **MacBook Air:** Ideal for students, casual users, web browsing, document editing, and light creative work.
- **MacBook Pro:** Suitable for professionals and power users who require high performance for tasks like video editing, programming, graphic design, and 3D modeling.

In summary, the choice between a MacBook Air and a MacBook Pro depends on your specific needs, budget, and performance requirements. The MacBook Air is excellent for everyday use and portability, while the MacBook Pro offers more power and features for demanding tasks but may come at a higher price point and with slightly reduced portability. As of my last update in September 2021, Apple has also introduced Apple Silicon-based MacBook Air and MacBook Pro models, which offer significant performance improvements and energy efficiency compared to their Intel-based counterparts. Be sure to consider the latest models and configurations when making your decision, as Apple regularly updates its product lineup.

Target audience and use cases for macbook air:

- **Students:** MacBook Air is an excellent choice for students due to its lightweight design, long battery life, and portability. It's ideal for taking to classes and libraries.
- **Casual Users:** If you primarily use your laptop for web browsing, social media, email, and streaming content, the MacBook Air offers more than enough performance.
- **Travelers:** Its slim profile and extended battery life make the MacBook Air an ideal travel companion. Whether you're on a plane or at a coffee shop, it's easy to carry.
- **Business Professionals:** If your work involves typical office tasks like word processing, spreadsheet management, and video conferencing, the MacBook Air can handle these efficiently.
- **Light Creative Work:** MacBook Air can handle light creative work like photo editing, graphic design, and casual video editing, especially in its Apple Silicon M1 versions, which offer improved graphics performance.
- **Budget-Conscious Users:** It's a more affordable MacBook option, making it suitable for users who want the macOS experience without breaking the bank.

Target Audience and Use Cases for MacBook Pro:

- **Creative Professionals:** MacBook Pro is favored by photographers, video editors, graphic designers, and music producers due to its powerful processors, accurate display, and ample RAM.

- **Software Developers:** For coding and software development, especially when working with resource-intensive applications, a MacBook Pro offers the performance needed for compiling code quickly and running virtual machines.
- **Professional Video Editors:** The 16-inch MacBook Pro, in particular, is a top choice for video editing professionals who require high-performance GPUs and a larger display.
- **3D Modelers and Animators:** Those working in 3D modeling, animation, and rendering software benefit from the MacBook Pro's powerful processors and dedicated GPUs.
- **Multitaskers:** If you regularly run multiple applications simultaneously or need to handle resource-intensive tasks, the MacBook Pro's higher processing power and RAM capacity are advantageous.
- **Gamers (M1 Pro and M1 Max Models):** The M1 Pro and M1 Max versions of the MacBook Pro offer improved gaming performance, making them suitable for gaming enthusiasts.
- **Anyone Needing Extensive Ports:** MacBook Pro models provide a variety of ports, including USB-C/Thunderbolt, HDMI, and MagSafe (in some models), making them suitable for connecting to a range of peripherals.
- **Prosumers:** Users who want a balance between performance and portability may opt for the 13-inch MacBook Pro, which offers more power than the MacBook Air without the bulk of the 16-inch model.

In summary, the choice between a MacBook Air and MacBook Pro depends on your specific needs and priorities. The MacBook Air excels in portability and is suitable for everyday tasks, while the MacBook Pro offers higher performance and is ideal for professionals and power users handling resource-intensive tasks. Consider your budget, performance requirements, and the nature of your work or usage when making your decision.

MACBOOK LINEUP OVERVIEW

As of my last knowledge update in September 2021, Apple's MacBook lineup encompassed a range of laptops designed to cater to diverse user needs, from everyday computing to professional-level tasks. While there may have been updates and new models introduced since then, I'll provide an overview of the major MacBook models available at that time.

MacBook Air:

- **Target Audience:** General consumers, students, and travelers.

Key Features:

- Ultra-thin and lightweight design, making it highly portable.
- Retina display for sharp visuals.
- Long battery life for all-day use.
- Typically features energy-efficient processors, such as Intel Core i3, i5, or i7 (before Apple Silicon M1).
- Excellent for web browsing, media consumption, and everyday tasks.
- Integrated Magic Keyboard and trackpad.
- Limited number of ports (USB-C/Thunderbolt).

MacBook Pro (13-inch):

- **Target Audience:** Professionals, students, and creatives seeking a balance between power and portability.

Key Features:
- Retina display with high resolution.
- More powerful processors compared to the MacBook Air.
- Suitable for tasks like video editing, software development, and graphic design.
- Robust build quality.
- Magic Keyboard.
- Various configurations available, including Intel and Apple Silicon (M1) models.
- A moderate number of ports, including Thunderbolt 3 (USB-C).

MacBook Pro (16-inch):

- **Target Audience:** Professional users requiring high performance and a larger display.

Key Features:
- Larger Retina display for enhanced productivity and content creation.
- Powerful processors, including Intel Core i5, i7, and i9 (in Intel-based models) or Apple Silicon M1 Pro and M1 Max (in Apple Silicon models).
- Ideal for demanding tasks such as 3D rendering, video production, and professional-grade software.
- Excellent audio quality with enhanced speakers.
- Larger chassis with more ports, including USB-C/Thunderbolt, HDMI, and MagSafe.
- Premium build quality and advanced thermal management.

MacBook (12-inch) [Discontinued]:
- **Target Audience:** Users who prioritize extreme portability.

Key Features:
- Ultra-slim and lightweight design.
- Retina display.
- Fanless design with low-power Intel processors.
- Single USB-C port for charging and connectivity.
- Limited processing power, suitable for basic tasks.

MacBook Air with Apple Silicon (M1):
- **Target Audience:** General consumers, students, and travelers.

Key Features:
- Similar to the Intel-based MacBook Air but powered by Apple's custom-designed M1 chip.
- Offers significant performance and efficiency improvements.
- Enhanced graphics and battery life.
- Runs both native M1 and Intel apps through Rosetta 2 translation.
- Retains the slim and lightweight design.

MacBook Pro with Apple Silicon (M1):

- **Target Audience:** Professionals and power users.

Key Features:
- Utilizes Apple's M1 chip for exceptional performance and energy efficiency.
- Significant gains in CPU and GPU performance.
- Excellent for tasks like video editing, software development, and more.
- Features the Magic Keyboard.
- Supports running both M1 and Intel apps through Rosetta 2.
- Limited port options (USB-C/Thunderbolt).

Please note that Apple regularly updates its MacBook lineup, and there may have been new releases and changes since my last knowledge update in September 2021. When considering a MacBook, it's crucial to assess your specific needs and budget and to research the latest models and configurations to make an informed choice.

CURRENT MODELS AND SPECIFICATIONS

As of my last knowledge update in September 2021, I can provide information on the MacBook models available at that time. However, please note that Apple frequently updates its product lineup, so it's essential to check the Apple website or other reliable sources for the most up-to-date information on current MacBook models and specifications. Here's an overview of the MacBook models available in 2021:

MacBook Air (M1, 2020):

- **Target Audience:** General consumers, students, and travelers.

Key Features:
- Powered by Apple's custom-designed M1 chip, offering remarkable performance and energy efficiency.
- Retina display with True Tone.
- Magic Keyboard.
- Silent operation due to fanless design.
- Excellent battery life.
- Available in 13-inch models with different storage and RAM configurations.
- USB-C/Thunderbolt 3 ports, headphone jack.

MacBook Pro 13-inch (M1, 2020):
- **Target Audience:** Professionals, students, and creatives requiring performance and portability.

Key Features:
- Powered by the Apple M1 chip for impressive performance improvements.
- Retina display with True Tone.
- Magic Keyboard.
- More power-efficient and silent compared to Intel-based predecessors.
- Available in various configurations with different storage and RAM options.
- USB-C/Thunderbolt 3 ports, headphone jack.

MacBook Pro 14-inch and 16-inch (2021):

- **Target Audience:** Professional users requiring high performance and a larger display.

Key Features:
- Powered by Apple's M1 Pro or M1 Max chips (varying by configuration).
- Larger Retina displays (14-inch or 16-inch) with ProMotion technology for smooth visuals.
- Magic Keyboard.
- Enhanced audio quality.
- A variety of configurations with high RAM and storage capacities.
- A range of ports, including USB-C/Thunderbolt 4, HDMI, and MagSafe (in some models).
- Advanced thermal management for sustained performance.

Please note that the information provided here is based on models available up to September 2021. Apple frequently updates its products, so the lineup and specifications may have changed since then. It's advisable to visit the official Apple website or consult a reliable source for the latest information on current MacBook models and their specifications. Additionally, Apple may have introduced new models or revisions after my last knowledge update.

**2.**

MACBOOK HARDWARE

MacBooks are known for their high-quality hardware, featuring a combination of cutting-edge technology and design aesthetics. Below, I'll provide an overview of the essential hardware components and features typically found in MacBooks:

Processor (CPU):
- MacBooks are powered by processors developed by Apple (Apple Silicon) or Intel (in older models).
- Apple Silicon chips, such as the M1, M1 Pro, and M1 Max, offer remarkable performance and energy efficiency, making them well-suited for a wide range of tasks.
- Processors determine a laptop's speed and ability to handle tasks, from web browsing to video editing.

Graphics Processing Unit (GPU):
- Apple's custom-designed GPUs (integrated graphics) are featured in most MacBook models.
- Some MacBook Pro models also offer dedicated GPUs for enhanced graphics performance, crucial for tasks like video editing, 3D rendering, and gaming.

Memory (RAM):
- RAM (Random Access Memory) affects a MacBook's multitasking capabilities.
- MacBooks typically offer RAM options ranging from 8GB to 64GB, depending on the model.
- More RAM allows for smoother multitasking and handling of memory-intensive applications.

Storage (SSD):
- MacBooks utilize Solid-State Drives (SSDs) for storage, which offers faster data access speeds and durability compared to traditional hard drives.
- Storage capacities can range from 256GB to several terabytes (TB), depending on the model.
- The choice of storage capacity should align with your needs for storing files, applications, and media.

Display:
- MacBooks come equipped with Retina displays, known for their high-resolution, sharp visuals, and accurate color reproduction.

- Various screen sizes are available, from 13 inches to 16 inches (as of my last knowledge update).
- Features like True Tone and ProMotion (higher refresh rates) enhance the visual experience.

Keyboard and Trackpad:
- Apple's Magic Keyboard is standard across MacBook models, offering comfortable and responsive typing.
- Multi-Touch trackpads provide precise cursor control and support gestures for easy navigation.

Ports and Connectivity:
- USB-C/Thunderbolt 3 or 4 ports are common in MacBooks, offering versatile connectivity for various peripherals and high-speed data transfer.
- Some models feature additional ports like HDMI, MagSafe (for charging), and SDXC card slots.

Battery:

- MacBooks are designed for long battery life, with models like the MacBook Air capable of providing all-day usage on a single charge.
- Battery life varies based on usage and the specific model.

Audio:
- MacBooks are equipped with stereo speakers for clear and immersive audio.
- Some MacBook Pro models feature enhanced speaker systems for even better sound quality.

Webcam and Microphone:
- MacBooks come with built-in webcams (FaceTime HD cameras) and microphones for video conferencing and recording.
- Recent models feature improved camera and microphone quality.

Security Features:
- Touch ID (or Face ID on newer models) provides biometric authentication for secure login and Apple Pay transactions.
- Apple's T2 or T1 security chip enhances data encryption and device security.

Thermal Design and Cooling:

- MacBook Pro models, especially the 16-inch version, have advanced thermal management systems to handle heat during intensive tasks.

Build Quality:
- MacBooks are known for their premium build quality, featuring aluminum unibody constructions that offer durability and aesthetics.

Ergonomics:

MacBooks are designed for comfort and ergonomics, with carefully placed keyboard, trackpad, and display for optimal user experience.

It's important to note that Apple regularly updates its MacBook lineup, introducing new hardware components and features to stay at the forefront of technology. When considering a MacBook, it's essential to assess your specific needs and budget, as well as the latest available models and configurations, to make an informed choice that aligns with your requirements.

COMPONENTS AND SPECIFICATIONS

MacBooks are renowned for their top-notch components and specifications, which contribute to their overall performance and user experience. Here's a detailed breakdown of the key components and specifications you'll find in a typical MacBook:

Processor (CPU):
- **Apple Silicon:** Apple-designed processors, such as the M1, M1 Pro, and M1 Max, offer impressive performance, energy efficiency, and compatibility with macOS. These chips power the latest MacBook models.
- **Intel:** Older MacBook models used Intel processors, which varied in terms of speed and performance. These models have been phased out in favor of Apple Silicon.

Graphics Processing Unit (GPU):
- **Integrated GPU:** Most MacBook models feature integrated Apple GPUs (Graphics Processing Units) for general graphics processing. Apple's GPUs provide excellent performance and efficiency.
- **Dedicated GPU:** Some MacBook Pro models offer dedicated GPUs from AMD or NVIDIA, which provide enhanced graphics performance for tasks like video editing and 3D rendering.

Memory (RAM):

- RAM (Random Access Memory) affects a MacBook's multitasking capabilities.

- MacBook models typically offer RAM options ranging from 8GB to 64GB, with some entry-level models starting at 8GB and high-end models providing more extensive memory for demanding tasks.

Storage (SSD):
- MacBooks utilize Solid-State Drives (SSDs) for storage, which offer faster data access speeds and durability compared to traditional hard drives.
- Storage capacities can range from 256GB to several terabytes (TB), depending on the model.
- The choice of storage capacity should align with your needs for storing files, applications, and media.

Display:
MacBooks are equipped with Retina displays known for their high-resolution, sharp visuals, and accurate color reproduction.
Various screen sizes are available, from 13 inches to 16 inches (as of my last knowledge update).
Features like True Tone and ProMotion (higher refresh rates) enhance the visual experience.

Ports and Connectivity:
USB-C/Thunderbolt 3 or 4 ports are common in MacBooks, offering versatile connectivity for various peripherals and high-speed data transfer.
Some models feature additional ports like HDMI, MagSafe (for charging), and SDXC card slots.

Battery:
MacBooks are designed for long battery life, with models like the MacBook Air capable of providing all-day usage on a single charge.
Battery life varies based on usage and the specific model.

Audio:
MacBooks are equipped with stereo speakers for clear and immersive audio.
Some MacBook Pro models feature enhanced speaker systems for even better sound quality.

Webcam and Microphone:
MacBooks come with built-in webcams (FaceTime HD cameras) and microphones for video conferencing and recording.
Recent models feature improved camera and microphone quality.

Security Features:
Touch ID (or Face ID on newer models) provides biometric authentication for secure login and Apple Pay transactions.
Apple's T2 or T1 security chip enhances data encryption and device security.

Thermal Design and Cooling:
MacBook Pro models, especially the 16-inch version, have advanced thermal management systems to handle heat during intensive tasks.

Build Quality:
MacBooks are known for their premium build quality, featuring aluminum unibody constructions that offer durability and aesthetics.

Ergonomics:
MacBooks are designed for comfort and ergonomics, with carefully placed keyboard, trackpad, and display for optimal user experience.

Operating System:
All MacBooks run macOS, Apple's operating system, known for its stability, security, and user-friendly interface.
These components and specifications come together to deliver a seamless and powerful computing experience on a MacBook. Keep in mind that Apple regularly updates its MacBook lineup, introducing new hardware components and features to stay at the forefront of technology. When considering a MacBook, it's essential to assess your specific needs and budget and to research the latest available models and configurations to make an informed choice that aligns with your requirements.

CPU, RAM, AND STORAGE OPTIONS

Certainly, let's dive deeper into the CPU, RAM (Random Access Memory), and storage options commonly found in MacBook laptops:

CPU (Central Processing Unit):
Apple Silicon CPUs (M1, M1 Pro, M1 Max):
Apple has transitioned to using its custom-designed CPUs, starting with the M1 chip and subsequent variations like M1 Pro and M1 Max in MacBook Pro models.
These CPUs are built on ARM architecture and feature a combination of high-performance and high-efficiency cores. The high-performance cores handle demanding tasks, while the high-efficiency cores conserve power during lighter workloads.
They provide excellent single-core and multi-core performance, making MacBooks with Apple Silicon among the fastest laptops available.
The M1 Pro and M1 Max offer even more CPU cores and GPU cores, making them suitable for demanding professional workloads.

Intel CPUs (in older MacBook models):
Older MacBook models used Intel processors, which varied in terms of performance depending on the specific chip used.
Intel CPUs offered configurations ranging from dual-core to quad-core, with clock speeds that determined how fast the CPU could execute instructions.
MacBooks with Intel CPUs were known for their compatibility with a wide range of software, including virtualization for running Windows and Linux.

RAM (Random Access Memory):
RAM Capacity:
RAM is a type of volatile memory used for temporarily storing data that is actively being used by the CPU.
MacBook models typically offer RAM options ranging from 8GB to 64GB.
More RAM allows for smoother multitasking and the ability to handle memory-intensive applications, such as video editing or running virtual machines.

MACBOOK GUIDE

RAM Type:
In MacBooks with Apple Silicon, LPDDR4X RAM is commonly used for its energy efficiency and high bandwidth.
In Intel-based MacBooks (older models), DDR4 or LPDDR3 RAM was used, depending on the specific model.

Storage (SSD - Solid-State Drive):
Storage Capacity:
MacBook laptops come with SSD storage, which is faster and more reliable than traditional hard drives.
Storage capacities can vary widely, ranging from 256GB to several terabytes (TB), depending on the MacBook model and configuration.
Consider your storage needs for apps, files, and media when choosing a capacity.

SSD Speed and Technology:
Apple uses custom-designed SSDs with controllers optimized for performance and reliability.
SSD speed is measured in terms of read and write speeds, with higher speeds leading to faster data access.
The latest MacBook models with Apple Silicon often feature extremely fast SSDs, resulting in quicker boot times, app loading, and file transfers.

Upgradeability:
Some MacBook models allow for user upgrades of storage, while others have soldered storage components, making upgrades impossible.
It's crucial to consider your long-term storage needs when selecting a MacBook model, as upgrading storage in non-user-upgradable models can be challenging or impossible.
In summary, the CPU, RAM, and storage options are critical factors to consider when choosing a MacBook. Apple's transition to custom-designed Apple Silicon processors has brought impressive performance and energy efficiency to its laptops. RAM capacity influences multitasking capabilities, and storage capacity and speed affect the laptop's overall performance and your ability to store and access data efficiently. Be sure to assess your specific needs and budget when selecting the right MacBook model and configuration.

GRAPHICS AND DISPLAY FEATURES

Graphics and display features are essential aspects of MacBook laptops, influencing visual quality, productivity, and overall user experience. Here's a comprehensive explanation of these components:

Graphics Processing Unit (GPU):
Integrated Apple GPU (Apple Silicon models):
MacBooks with Apple Silicon (M1, M1 Pro, M1 Max) feature integrated Apple GPUs.
These GPUs are part of the system-on-chip (SoC) design, providing excellent graphics performance for everyday tasks, creative work, and even light gaming.
Apple's GPUs are highly power-efficient and optimized for macOS, ensuring smooth graphics rendering while conserving battery life.

The M1 Pro and M1 Max models offer dedicated GPU cores for enhanced graphics performance, making them suitable for demanding professional tasks like video editing and 3D rendering.

Dedicated GPUs (Intel-based MacBook Pro models, some older models):

Some MacBook Pro models used dedicated GPUs from AMD or NVIDIA in the past.

Dedicated GPUs provide more substantial graphics processing power, making them ideal for graphics-intensive applications, including gaming and professional content creation.

While dedicated GPUs offer superior performance, they may consume more power and generate more heat.

Display Features:

Retina Display:

Retina displays are a hallmark of MacBook laptops, known for their high resolution and pixel density, resulting in sharp and clear visuals.

Retina displays offer excellent color accuracy and contrast, making them suitable for tasks like photo and video editing, graphic design, and content consumption.

The term "Retina" signifies that the pixel density is high enough that individual pixels are not easily distinguishable from a normal viewing distance.

True Tone:

True Tone is a display technology that adjusts the color temperature of the screen based on the ambient lighting conditions.

This feature ensures that the screen appears more natural and comfortable to the eyes, reducing strain in various lighting environments.

ProMotion (High Refresh Rate):

Some MacBook models feature ProMotion technology, which provides a higher refresh rate, typically up to 120Hz.

A higher refresh rate results in smoother scrolling, reduced motion blur, and improved responsiveness when interacting with the screen.

ProMotion is particularly beneficial for tasks like video editing, 3D modeling, and gaming.

Size and Resolution:

MacBook laptops come in various screen sizes, ranging from 13 inches to 16 inches (as of my last knowledge update).

The size you choose depends on your preferences and requirements, with larger screens offering more screen real estate for multitasking and content creation.

The resolution varies across models but generally provides excellent clarity and detail.

HDR (High Dynamic Range):

Some MacBook models support High Dynamic Range (HDR), enhancing the range between the darkest and brightest colors on the screen.

HDR content appears more vivid and lifelike, making it suitable for media consumption and creative work.

P3 Wide Color Gamut:

MacBook displays often cover the P3 wide color gamut, which means they can reproduce a broader range of colors compared to standard displays.

This feature is crucial for professional tasks like photo and video editing, where color accuracy is paramount.

Anti-Reflective Coating:
Many MacBook displays have an anti-reflective coating that reduces glare and minimizes reflections, improving visibility in various lighting conditions.
In conclusion, graphics and display features on MacBook laptops are designed to provide stunning visuals, color accuracy, and an immersive user experience. Whether you're a creative professional, a casual user, or a gamer, MacBook displays cater to a wide range of needs, while integrated and dedicated GPUs ensure smooth graphics performance for your specific tasks. When choosing a MacBook, consider your requirements for graphics capabilities and display features to select the best model for your needs.

PORTS AND CONNECTIVITY

Ports and connectivity options on MacBook laptops play a crucial role in connecting to peripherals, transferring data, and expanding functionality. Here's a comprehensive explanation of the most common ports and connectivity features found on MacBooks:

USB-C/Thunderbolt 3 and Thunderbolt 4 Ports:

| Thunderbolt 4 | Thunderbolt 3 | USB-C | USB4 |

- **USB-C:** Many MacBook models feature USB-C ports, which are versatile and reversible, allowing you to connect a wide range of devices, including external hard drives, displays, docking stations, and more.
- **Thunderbolt 3:** Some USB-C ports on MacBooks are Thunderbolt 3 ports. Thunderbolt 3 provides even faster data transfer speeds (up to 40Gbps) and supports connecting to high-resolution displays and external GPUs (eGPUs).
- **Thunderbolt 4:** Thunderbolt 4 is an updated version of Thunderbolt 3, offering the same 40Gbps data transfer speeds but with additional features like better power delivery and improved support for docks and peripherals.
- **Daisy-Chaining:** Thunderbolt ports allow for daisy-chaining, where you can connect multiple Thunderbolt devices in a series, simplifying cable management and reducing clutter.

HDMI Port:
Some MacBook models, particularly the MacBook Pro, come equipped with an HDMI (High-Definition Multimedia Interface) port.
HDMI ports allow you to connect your MacBook to external displays, projectors, or HDTVs without the need for adapters or dongles.
This is useful for presentations, content sharing, and enjoying media on a larger screen.

MagSafe (Not on all models):
MagSafe is a proprietary magnetic charging connector used in older MacBook models (pre-2016).
It ensures a secure and easily detachable connection for charging your MacBook.
Newer MacBook models have transitioned to USB-C for charging.

3.5mm Headphone Jack:
Most MacBook models include a 3.5mm headphone jack for connecting headphones, external speakers, or audio equipment.
This standard audio port is useful for listening to music, watching videos, or engaging in virtual meetings.

SDXC Card Slot (Select MacBook Pro models):
Some MacBook Pro models come with an SDXC card slot, which is handy for photographers and videographers who need to transfer media files from cameras and other SD card-based devices.

Wi-Fi and Bluetooth:
All MacBooks are equipped with Wi-Fi and Bluetooth connectivity.
The latest MacBook models support Wi-Fi 6 (802.11ax) for faster wireless internet speeds and improved connectivity in crowded environments.
Bluetooth allows you to connect wireless peripherals such as a mouse, keyboard, headphones, or speakers.

FaceTime HD Camera and Microphones:
MacBooks come with built-in FaceTime HD cameras and microphones for video conferencing, online meetings, and video recording.
Newer models offer improved camera and microphone quality for better video and audio communication.

Wireless Options:
MacBooks support wireless technologies like AirDrop for easy file sharing between Apple devices, AirPlay for streaming content to compatible displays, and Handoff for seamless continuity between your MacBook and other Apple devices.

Ethernet (via USB-C or Thunderbolt Adapter):
For wired network connectivity, you can use a USB-C or Thunderbolt adapter to connect to Ethernet.
This is useful for users who require a stable and high-speed internet connection in specific scenarios.

Expansion and Docking Stations:

If you need additional ports and connectivity options, you can invest in docking stations or hubs that connect to your MacBook via USB-C or Thunderbolt.

These devices provide a range of ports, including USB-A, HDMI, Ethernet, and more, to expand your MacBook's capabilities.

In summary, MacBook laptops offer a mix of modern and versatile ports and connectivity options that cater to various user needs. The transition to USB-C/Thunderbolt 3 and 4 has made connectivity more flexible and compatible with a wide range of peripherals. It's essential to consider your specific requirements for ports and connectivity when selecting a MacBook model and, if necessary, invest in adapters or docking solutions to meet your connectivity needs.

USB-C, THUNDERBOLT, AND OTHER PORTS

USB-C and Thunderbolt are two of the most important and versatile port technologies found on modern MacBook laptops, offering various functionalities for connecting peripherals, data transfer, and charging. Additionally, there are other ports that may be present on some MacBook models. Here's a detailed explanation of these por

USB-C (USB Type-C):
- **USB-C is a reversible and versatile connector:** It can be inserted into the port in either orientation, eliminating the frustration of trying to plug it in the right way.
- **Compatibility:** USB-C is a universal standard used across various devices, including laptops, smartphones, tablets, and accessories.
- **Data Transfer:** USB-C ports support high-speed data transfer rates, depending on the generation (USB 3.1 Gen 1, Gen 2, or USB 4). Data can be transferred to and from external hard drives, flash drives, and more.
- **Charging:** USB-C can provide power to devices and charge your MacBook. USB-C Power Delivery (PD) is a standard that allows fast charging and is commonly used in MacBook power adapters.
- **Video Output:** USB-C supports video output to external monitors and displays. With the right adapter or cable, you can connect your MacBook to HDMI, DisplayPort, or VGA displays.
- **Audio:** USB-C can carry audio signals for headphones, speakers, and microphones.
- **Accessories:** Many peripherals and accessories, such as hubs, docking stations, and external SSDs, use USB-C connections.
- **Thunderbolt 3 and 4:** Some USB-C ports are also Thunderbolt 3 or Thunderbolt 4 ports, which offer additional features like faster data transfer, support for high-resolution displays, and daisy-chaining multiple devices.

Thunderbolt (Thunderbolt 3 and Thunderbolt 4):

Thunderbolt is an advanced technology built on the USB-C physical connector. It offers higher data transfer speeds and more capabilities than standard USB-C.
- **Data Transfer:** Thunderbolt 3 and 4 provide extremely high data transfer rates, up to 40Gbps (Thunderbolt 3) and 40Gbps (Thunderbolt 4).
- **Video Output:** Thunderbolt supports connecting multiple high-resolution displays (including 4K and 5K monitors) through a single port.

- **Daisy-Chaining:** Thunderbolt allows you to daisy-chain multiple Thunderbolt devices together, simplifying cable management.
- **Power Delivery:** Thunderbolt ports can deliver significant power to connected devices, including laptops, monitors, and peripherals.
- **External GPUs (eGPUs):** Thunderbolt is commonly used to connect external graphics cards, which can boost a MacBook's graphics performance for tasks like gaming and 3D rendering.
- **Compatibility:** Thunderbolt 3 and 4 ports are also compatible with USB-C devices. However, not all USB-C ports are Thunderbolt-compatible.

HDMI Port:
HDMI (High-Definition Multimedia Interface) ports are used to connect MacBooks to external displays, projectors, or HDTVs.
HDMI provides high-quality video and audio output, making it ideal for presentations, media playback, and extending your MacBook's display.

MagSafe (Not on all models):
MagSafe is a magnetic charging connector used in older MacBook models (pre-2016).
It ensures a secure and easily detachable connection for charging your MacBook.
Newer MacBook models have transitioned to USB-C for charging.

3.5mm Headphone Jack:
The 3.5mm headphone jack allows you to connect headphones, external speakers, or audio equipment to your MacBook.
It provides standard audio output and input for listening to music, watching videos, and conducting audio calls.
These ports and connectors are essential for expanding your MacBook's capabilities and connecting to various peripherals. When choosing a MacBook model, consider your specific needs for ports and connectivity, especially if you rely on specific accessories or require certain features like high-speed data transfer or external display support. If necessary, adapters and docking stations can help bridge the gap between your MacBook and devices that use different connectors.

WI-FI AND BLUETOOTH

Wi-Fi and Bluetooth are two wireless communication technologies that play integral roles in MacBook laptops, providing connectivity to networks, peripherals, and other devices. Here's a comprehensive explanation of both technologies:

Wi-Fi (Wireless Fidelity):
- **Purpose:** Wi-Fi enables wireless internet connectivity, allowing your MacBook to connect to Wi-Fi networks, including home networks, public hotspots, and corporate networks.
- **Standards:** MacBooks support various Wi-Fi standards, with the latest models typically featuring Wi-Fi 6 (802.11ax). Older models may support Wi-Fi 5 (802.11ac) or earlier standards.

- **Speed and Range:** Wi-Fi standards determine the speed and range of wireless connections. Newer standards offer faster data transfer speeds and improved range, resulting in better performance and coverage.
- **Dual-Band Wi-Fi:** Many MacBooks support dual-band Wi-Fi, which operates on both 2.4GHz and 5GHz frequency bands. This provides flexibility in choosing the best frequency for a given situation, as 5GHz is less crowded and offers faster speeds but has shorter range.
- **MIMO (Multiple Input, Multiple Output):** MacBooks often feature MIMO technology, which uses multiple antennas to improve signal quality and throughput.
- **Security:** Wi-Fi networks can be secured using various encryption protocols like WPA3, ensuring data transmitted between your MacBook and the router is encrypted and protected from unauthorized access.
- **Network Types:** MacBooks can connect to different types of Wi-Fi networks, including open networks, WPA/WPA2/WPA3-protected networks, and enterprise networks with advanced security configurations.
- **Wi-Fi Assist:** macOS includes a feature called Wi-Fi Assist, which automatically switches between Wi-Fi and cellular data when the Wi-Fi signal is weak, ensuring a seamless internet connection.

Bluetooth:
- **Purpose:** Bluetooth is a short-range wireless technology primarily used for connecting your MacBook to various peripherals and devices without the need for cables.
- **Peripheral Connectivity:** Bluetooth enables connections to devices such as wireless mice, keyboards, headphones, speakers, printers, and smartphones.
- **Bluetooth Versions:** MacBooks support various Bluetooth versions, with the latest models typically featuring Bluetooth 5.0 or newer. Each version introduces improvements in range, data transfer speeds, and energy efficiency.
- **Bluetooth LE (Low Energy):** Bluetooth LE is a variant of Bluetooth designed for devices that require minimal power consumption, such as fitness trackers and smartwatches. It allows these devices to operate for extended periods on small batteries.
- **Pairing:** To connect your MacBook to a Bluetooth device, you typically pair them by putting the device into pairing mode and selecting it in your MacBook's Bluetooth settings.
- **Audio Connectivity:** Bluetooth is commonly used for wireless audio, allowing you to connect wireless headphones, earbuds, or speakers to your MacBook for music, video calls, and more.
- **File Transfer:** Bluetooth can also be used for file transfer between devices. On a MacBook, you can use Bluetooth to send files to other Bluetooth-enabled devices.
- **Compatibility:** Bluetooth is a universal standard supported by a wide range of devices and platforms, making it versatile for connecting to various peripherals.

Both Wi-Fi and Bluetooth are crucial for the wireless functionality and connectivity of MacBook laptops. They enhance your MacBook's usability by enabling internet access, seamless communication with peripherals, and connections to other devices in your ecosystem. It's important to keep your Wi-Fi and Bluetooth drivers and software up to date to ensure optimal performance and security.

INPUT DEVICES

Input devices on a MacBook are essential components that allow you to interact with the computer and provide input in various forms. Here's a comprehensive explanation of the key input devices commonly found on MacBook laptops:

Keyboard:
The keyboard is the primary input device on a MacBook, used for typing text, entering commands, and executing various functions.
MacBook keyboards are known for their slim design and tactile feedback.
Recent MacBook models feature the Magic Keyboard, which offers a comfortable typing experience with a scissor mechanism and improved key stability.
Some MacBook Pro models also include a Touch Bar, a touch-sensitive OLED strip above the keyboard that provides context-aware functions and controls.

Trackpad:
The trackpad is a large, multi-touch input device that serves as the MacBook's primary pointing device.
It allows for precise cursor control, gestures (like scrolling, zooming, and swiping), and clicking.
MacBook trackpads support Force Touch, which can detect different levels of pressure, enabling actions like "Quick Look" or previewing links.

Touch Bar (on some MacBook Pro models):

The Touch Bar is a touch-sensitive OLED display located above the keyboard on certain MacBook Pro models.
It offers context-aware controls and shortcuts that change depending on the active application.
The Touch Bar allows for quick access to functions, such as adjusting volume, brightness, and media playback controls.

Touch ID (on some MacBook models):
Touch ID is a fingerprint sensor integrated into the power button (or near the keyboard) on certain MacBook models.
It provides biometric authentication, allowing you to unlock your MacBook, make secure payments with Apple Pay, and authenticate password-protected apps.

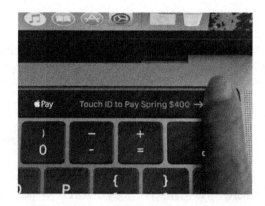

External Input Devices:
MacBooks can be connected to a variety of external input devices, including mice and graphics tablets, for specialized tasks such as graphic design, 3D modeling, and gaming.
Apple's Magic Mouse and Magic Trackpad are popular external input devices designed to work seamlessly with MacBooks.

Voice Input:
MacBooks support voice input and voice commands through Siri, Apple's voice-activated assistant.
You can use Siri to perform tasks, open applications, find information, and more using natural language.

Built-in Microphone:
MacBook laptops include a built-in microphone for audio input, enabling you to make voice calls, record audio, and use voice recognition features.

External Keyboards and Mice:
Many users prefer external keyboards and mice for specific tasks or ergonomic reasons.
USB or Bluetooth keyboards and mice from various manufacturers are compatible with MacBooks.

Graphics Tablets:
Graphic designers and digital artists often use graphics tablets, like those from Wacom, for precise input when creating digital artwork or illustrations.
These tablets use a stylus or pen for drawing and offer pressure sensitivity.

Gaming Controllers:
MacBooks can connect to a variety of gaming controllers for playing games. Apple's macOS and third-party apps support various gamepads.

Accessibility Devices:
MacBooks provide accessibility features for individuals with disabilities, including support for braille displays, switch control devices, and alternative input methods.
In summary, input devices on a MacBook are crucial for interacting with the computer, whether you're typing, navigating the operating system, creating digital art, or playing games. Apple continually innovates in this area, offering comfortable and versatile input options to suit various user preferences and needs.

KEYBOARD AND TRACKPAD

Certainly, let's take a closer look at the keyboard and trackpad on MacBook laptops, two of the most crucial input devices that greatly influence the overall user experience:

Keyboard:
Design and Feel:
Apple's keyboards on MacBook laptops are known for their sleek and minimalist design.
They feature a low-profile scissor-switch mechanism that offers a balance between key travel (the distance a key moves when pressed) and tactile feedback (the sensation of pressing a key).
MacBook keyboards are designed for quiet and comfortable typing, making them suitable for extended use.

Key Features:
The key layout follows the standard QWERTY configuration, with a row of function keys (F1 to F12) at the top.
MacBook keyboards also include special keys like Command (⌘), Option (⌥), Control (^), and the Esc key, which are integral to macOS functions and keyboard shortcuts.
Recent MacBook models, particularly those with the Magic Keyboard, offer a dedicated Touch ID sensor for biometric authentication.

Backlighting:
MacBook keyboards feature adjustable backlighting that automatically adjusts to ambient lighting conditions.
This ensures that keys are visible in both well-lit and dim environments, enhancing usability in various settings.

Key Travel and Feedback:
Apple carefully engineers the key travel distance and force required to press a key, resulting in a comfortable typing experience.
The keys provide a satisfying tactile feedback without being too loud or requiring excessive force.

Key Durability:
Apple keyboards are designed for durability, with mechanisms rated for millions of keystrokes.
The materials used are resistant to wear and staining, helping to maintain the keyboard's appearance over time.

Trackpad:

Multi-Touch Trackpad:
The MacBook trackpad is a spacious, multi-touch input device that allows for precise cursor control and supports a wide range of multi-touch gestures.
Multi-touch gestures include scrolling, zooming, rotating, swiping, and more, making it intuitive to navigate macOS and interact with applications.

Force Touch:
Many MacBook models feature Force Touch technology, which can detect different levels of pressure applied to the trackpad's surface.
Force Touch enables actions like previewing files or web links, and it provides haptic feedback (a tactile response) when you press harder.

Palm Rejection:
MacBook trackpads employ palm rejection technology to prevent accidental touch inputs while typing.
This feature ensures that your palms and wrists don't interfere with trackpad operations while you're typing.

Large Surface Area:
MacBook trackpads are generously sized to provide ample space for gestures, making it easy to perform tasks like mission control, launching Launchpad, and accessing notification center with ease.

Glass Surface:
The trackpad's surface is made of glass, providing a smooth and responsive feel while also being resistant to wear and scratching.

Precision and Accuracy:
MacBook trackpads are renowned for their precision and accuracy, making them ideal for tasks that require fine control, such as graphic design or photo editing.
In summary, the keyboard and trackpad on MacBook laptops are meticulously designed to offer a comfortable and productive user experience. The keyboard provides tactile feedback and a quiet typing experience, while the trackpad offers precise control and supports a wide range of gestures for efficient navigation and interaction with macOS and applications. These input devices are integral to the MacBook's usability and contribute to its reputation for user-friendly design and functionality.

TOUCH BAR (IF APPLICABLE)

The Touch Bar is a unique input feature introduced by Apple on select MacBook Pro models. It's a touch-sensitive OLED display strip located above the traditional keyboard on the MacBook Pro. While not available on all MacBook models, the Touch Bar brings a dynamic and context-aware element to the keyboard area.

Here's a detailed explanation of the Touch Bar:

Design and Location:
The Touch Bar is a thin OLED touchscreen that spans the width of the keyboard on MacBook Pro models that include it.
It replaces the traditional function keys (F1 to F12) with a customizable, touch-sensitive strip.

Dynamic and Context-Aware:
The primary feature of the Touch Bar is its adaptability and context-awareness. It displays controls and shortcuts that are relevant to the active application or task.
For example, when using Safari, the Touch Bar may show website shortcuts, tab management controls, and a search bar. In the Photos app, it can display photo editing tools and filters.

Customization:
Users can customize the Touch Bar's contents to some extent. You can add, remove, and rearrange shortcuts and controls in the Touch Bar, tailoring it to your preferences and workflow.

Touch ID Integration:
Some MacBook Pro models with the Touch Bar include a Touch ID sensor, located on the far right side of the bar.
Touch ID allows you to securely unlock your MacBook, make Apple Pay transactions, and authenticate password-protected apps and tasks.

Keyboard and System Controls:
In addition to application-specific controls, the Touch Bar also provides standard keyboard functions such as adjusting brightness, volume, and media playback.
You can also use the Touch Bar to access system functions like Siri, Launchpad, and the Control Center.

Third-Party App Support:

Many third-party applications have integrated support for the Touch Bar. Popular software like Microsoft Office, Adobe Creative Cloud, and Final Cut Pro offer Touch Bar enhancements. This integration can streamline workflows and make certain tasks more efficient.

Dynamic Typing and Predictive Text:
When typing, the Touch Bar provides predictive text suggestions and autocorrect options, similar to the on-screen keyboard on iOS devices.
This can help improve typing speed and accuracy.

Accessibility:
The Touch Bar includes accessibility features like VoiceOver, which provides spoken feedback for visually impaired users.
It also supports the use of VoiceOver gestures for navigation.

Criticism and Controversy:
The Touch Bar has been a subject of debate among users and professionals. Some find it a valuable tool for productivity, while others consider it less useful than physical function keys.
Its absence in the latest MacBook Pro models (as of my last knowledge update) indicates a shift in Apple's approach to laptop design.
In summary, the Touch Bar is an innovative and context-aware input feature available on select MacBook Pro models. It aims to provide a dynamic and adaptive interface for various tasks and applications, enhancing productivity and convenience for users. While it has garnered both praise and criticism, its inclusion or omission depends on individual preferences and work requirements.

EXTERNAL PERIPHERALS

External peripherals refer to additional devices and accessories that can be connected to a MacBook to expand its capabilities, functionality, and versatility. These peripherals serve various purposes and cater to a wide range of user needs.

Here's a comprehensive explanation of common external peripherals for MacBooks:

External Displays:
External monitors or displays allow you to extend your MacBook's screen real estate for multitasking, improve productivity, and enjoy content on a larger screen.

You can connect an external display using the MacBook's HDMI, Thunderbolt, or USB-C ports, depending on the display's compatibility.

Professional users often opt for high-resolution and color-accurate displays for tasks like graphic design and video editing.

External Storage Devices:

External hard drives, solid-state drives (SSDs), and network-attached storage (NAS) devices provide additional storage space for data backup, file storage, and content creation.

These peripherals connect to your MacBook via USB, Thunderbolt, or network connections, depending on the device.

External Keyboards and Mice:

Some users prefer external keyboards and mice for ergonomic reasons or specific tasks.

Apple's Magic Keyboard and Magic Mouse are popular options, but you can also choose from a wide range of third-party options, including mechanical keyboards and gaming mice.

Docking Stations and Hubs:

Docking stations and hubs offer a variety of ports, including USB, HDMI, Ethernet, and SD card slots, to expand your MacBook's connectivity options.

They are particularly useful for MacBook models with limited ports, such as the MacBook Air.

Some docking stations also support multiple displays, allowing you to connect multiple monitors.

External Graphics Processing Units (eGPUs):

eGPUs are used by creative professionals and gamers to enhance graphics performance on their MacBook.

They connect via Thunderbolt and allow you to run graphics-intensive applications and games with improved performance.

Printers and Scanners:

You can connect a wide range of printers and scanners to your MacBook for document printing, photo printing, and scanning needs.

Most modern printers offer wireless connectivity for hassle-free printing.

External Audio Equipment:
Musicians and audio professionals often use external audio interfaces, MIDI controllers, microphones, and studio monitors to enhance audio recording and production on their MacBook.
USB and Thunderbolt connections are common for audio peripherals.

Webcams:
While MacBooks come with built-in FaceTime HD cameras, some users opt for external webcams for higher quality video conferencing and streaming.
USB webcams are widely compatible with MacBooks.

External DVD/Blu-ray Drives:
MacBook laptops no longer include built-in optical drives. If you need to read or write DVDs or Blu-ray discs, you can connect an external drive via USB or Thunderbolt.

Drawing Tablets and Graphics Pen Displays:
Graphic designers and digital artists often use drawing tablets and graphics pen displays for precise input and digital art creation.
These peripherals connect to your MacBook via USB or other compatible ports.

UPS (Uninterruptible Power Supply):
A UPS is a backup power supply that provides emergency power to your MacBook and peripherals during a power outage, preventing data loss and allowing for a safe shutdown.

Network Devices:
Ethernet switches, Wi-Fi routers, and access points can be used to extend your network coverage or improve wired and wireless connectivity.

External Batteries and Power Banks:
Portable chargers and external battery packs allow you to charge your MacBook and other devices on the go, extending your laptop's battery life.
These external peripherals expand the capabilities of your MacBook, allowing you to customize your setup according to your needs. Whether you're a professional looking for enhanced productivity or a hobbyist with specific requirements, there's a wide range of peripherals available to complement your MacBook and improve your overall computing experience.

3.

MACBOOK OPERATING SYSTEM

The MacBook operating system, officially known as macOS (formerly Mac OS X and OS X), is Apple's desktop and laptop computer operating system. macOS is designed to provide a seamless and user-friendly computing experience on MacBook laptops and Mac desktops. Here's a comprehensive explanation of macOS:

User Interface:
macOS features an intuitive and aesthetically pleasing user interface (UI) characterized by its clean design, smooth animations, and a user-friendly layout.
The Dock, located at the bottom of the screen, provides quick access to frequently used applications and files.
macOS supports multiple desktops (Spaces) and Mission Control, which help users manage and organize open windows and applications.

Security:
macOS emphasizes security and privacy. It includes features like Gatekeeper, which verifies the authenticity of applications, and FileVault, which encrypts your data.
Safari, the default web browser, incorporates robust privacy features and enhanced tracking prevention.
Apple's T2 and M1 security chips provide hardware-level security for data encryption and secure boot.

App Store:
The Mac App Store offers a wide range of applications and software, including productivity tools, games, and creative applications.

Apps from the App Store are vetted for security and compatibility with macOS.

Software Updates:
macOS receives regular updates that introduce new features, improvements, and security patches.
Users can easily update their macOS version through the App Store or System Preferences.

Compatibility:
macOS is designed to run on Apple hardware, including MacBook laptops and Mac desktops.
It supports both Intel-based Macs and Apple Silicon Macs, ensuring compatibility across a range of devices.

Integration with Apple Ecosystem:
macOS seamlessly integrates with other Apple devices and services, such as iPhone, iPad, Apple Watch, iCloud, and Apple Music.
Features like Handoff, Continuity, and Universal Clipboard allow for smooth transitions between devices.

Siri:
macOS includes Siri, Apple's voice-activated assistant, for performing tasks, answering questions, and controlling your MacBook using voice commands.

Time Machine:
Time Machine is a built-in backup and recovery solution that allows users to back up their entire macOS system, ensuring data safety and easy recovery.

Accessibility:
macOS offers a wide range of accessibility features to support users with disabilities, including VoiceOver, Magnifier, and more.

Developers and Creatives:
macOS is a preferred choice for developers, creatives, and professionals. It provides a Unix-based terminal for development, support for programming languages like Swift and Python, and creative tools like Final Cut Pro and Logic Pro.

Virtual Desktops:
macOS supports multiple virtual desktops (Spaces) and Mission Control, allowing users to organize and manage their workspace effectively.

Compatibility with Windows:
macOS includes Boot Camp, a utility that allows users to install and run Windows alongside macOS on Intel-based Macs.
With Apple Silicon Macs, you can use virtualization software like Parallels Desktop or VMware Fusion to run Windows applications within macOS.

Performance:
macOS is optimized for performance and efficiency, ensuring that MacBook laptops deliver smooth and responsive user experiences.

Continual Evolution:
Apple regularly releases new versions of macOS with feature updates and improvements, ensuring that the operating system remains up to date with the latest technology trends.
Overall, macOS is a robust and user-friendly operating system that provides a stable and secure computing environment for MacBook users. Its seamless integration with the Apple ecosystem, focus on security and privacy, and extensive software library make it a preferred choice for a wide range of users, from professionals to creative artists and casual users.

macOS OVERVIEW

macOS is Apple's desktop and laptop computer operating system, designed to provide a user-friendly and efficient computing experience on MacBook laptops, Mac desktops, and Mac Mini computers. It is known for its sleek and intuitive user interface, robust security features, and seamless integration with the Apple ecosystem. Here is a comprehensive overview of macOS:

User Interface and Design:
macOS features a visually appealing and user-friendly interface known for its clean, minimalistic design.
The Dock, located at the bottom of the screen, provides quick access to frequently used applications and folders.
The Menu Bar at the top of the screen displays essential system information, including the date and time, Wi-Fi status, and system notifications.

System Updates:

macOS receives regular updates that introduce new features, enhancements, and security patches.

Users can easily update their macOS version through the App Store or System Preferences.

App Store:

The Mac App Store is a platform where users can download a wide range of applications and software, including productivity tools, games, creative applications, and utilities.

Apps from the App Store are vetted for security and compatibility with macOS.

Security and Privacy:

macOS places a strong emphasis on security and user privacy.

Features like Gatekeeper verify the authenticity of applications, ensuring they come from trusted sources.

FileVault offers full-disk encryption to protect user data.

Safari, the default web browser, includes robust privacy features, such as Intelligent Tracking Prevention.

Compatibility and Hardware:

macOS is designed to run on Apple hardware, including MacBook laptops, Mac desktops, and Mac Mini computers.

It supports both Intel-based Macs and Apple Silicon Macs, ensuring a smooth transition for users.

Apple continually updates macOS to leverage the latest hardware advancements.

Integration with Apple Ecosystem:

macOS seamlessly integrates with other Apple devices and services, such as iPhone, iPad, Apple Watch, iCloud, and Apple Music.

What Is The Apple Ecosystem?

iBoysoft

Features like Handoff, Continuity, and Universal Clipboard allow for seamless transitions between devices.

Siri:

Siri, Apple's voice-activated assistant, is integrated into macOS, enabling users to perform tasks, find information, and control their Mac using voice commands.

Time Machine:

Time Machine is a built-in backup and recovery solution that simplifies data backup and ensures easy recovery of files and system states.

Accessibility:
macOS includes a comprehensive set of accessibility features to support users with disabilities. These features include VoiceOver, Magnifier, and more.

Developer Tools:
macOS is a preferred platform for developers and creatives, providing a Unix-based terminal, support for programming languages like Swift and Python, and a range of development tools. Xcode, Apple's integrated development environment (IDE), is widely used for macOS and iOS app development.

Virtual Desktops:
macOS offers multiple virtual desktops (Spaces) and Mission Control, allowing users to organize and manage their workspace efficiently.

Continual Evolution:
Apple regularly releases new versions of macOS with feature updates and improvements, ensuring that the operating system remains up to date with the latest technology trends.
In summary, macOS is a sophisticated and user-centric operating system that provides a stable and secure computing environment for a wide range of users, from professionals and developers to creative artists and everyday users. Its emphasis on design, security, and integration with the Apple ecosystem makes it a key element of the Apple computing experience.

LATEST VERSION AND UPDATES

As of my last knowledge update in September 2021, the latest version of macOS was macOS Monterey (version 12.0), which was announced at Apple's Worldwide Developers Conference (WWDC) in June 2021. Please note that there may have been subsequent macOS releases and updates since then. To get the most current information about macOS versions and updates, I recommend visiting Apple's official website or checking your MacBook's software updates.

However, I can provide a general overview of how macOS updates typically work:

Major macOS Releases:
Apple typically announces major macOS updates at its annual WWDC event in June.
These major releases introduce new features, enhancements, and improvements to the operating system.

macOS updates often have names inspired by California locations, such as Big Sur, Catalina, and Monterey.

Software Updates:
After the initial announcement, macOS updates go through several beta testing phases, during which developers and beta testers can try out the new features and report bugs.
Once the testing is complete and any issues have been resolved, Apple releases the new macOS version to the general public.

Availability:
macOS updates are typically available as free downloads from the Mac App Store or directly from the System Preferences > Software Update menu.
Users can choose to install the update when it becomes available.

Feature Highlights:
Each major macOS release comes with a set of feature highlights, which may include improvements in areas like user interface design, performance, security, and app functionality.
macOS updates often integrate new features that enhance the user experience and provide greater compatibility with other Apple devices and services.

Security and Bug Fixes:
macOS updates also include important security patches and bug fixes to address vulnerabilities and issues identified in previous versions.
Regularly updating your macOS is crucial for maintaining the security and stability of your MacBook.

Compatibility:
Apple strives to ensure that macOS updates are compatible with a range of Mac computers, but older Macs may not support the latest features.
Users are encouraged to check Apple's official website for compatibility information before updating.

Incremental Updates:
In addition to major macOS releases, Apple often releases incremental updates (e.g., 12.1, 12.2) throughout the year to address specific issues or add smaller enhancements.
These updates can be installed through the Software Update feature in System Preferences.

Automatic Updates:
Users can enable automatic macOS updates to ensure that their MacBook is always running the latest software version with the latest features, bug fixes, and security patches.
Please note that macOS updates are essential for keeping your MacBook secure and up to date with the latest features and improvements. It's generally recommended to keep your macOS installation current to benefit from these enhancements and ensure the best possible user experience.

USER INTERFACE AND FEATURES

The macOS user interface (UI) is known for its elegant design, user-friendly layout, and intuitive features. It's a key aspect of the macOS experience on MacBook laptops and Mac desktops. Here's a comprehensive explanation of the macOS user interface and its prominent features:

Desktop and Dock:

The macOS desktop is the primary workspace, where you can organize files, folders, and shortcuts. It features a clean and uncluttered design.

The Dock, located at the bottom of the screen, provides quick access to frequently used applications and folders. You can customize it by adding or removing app icons.

Finder:

Finder is the macOS file management application that allows users to browse, organize, and manipulate files and folders.

It features a sidebar for quick access to commonly used locations, a preview pane, and various view options.

Menu Bar:

The Menu Bar, located at the top of the screen, provides access to essential system functions and controls, including the date and time, Wi-Fi status, battery life (on laptops), volume controls, and system notifications.

It also displays the active application's menu, allowing users to access its features and settings.

System Preferences:

System Preferences is the control center for customizing and configuring macOS settings. It's accessible from the Menu Bar or the Dock.

Users can adjust system preferences related to displays, sound, network, privacy, accessibility, and more.

Spotlight Search:

Spotlight is a powerful search tool accessible from the Menu Bar. It allows users to search for files, apps, documents, emails, and more.
It also provides real-time information, such as weather, stock prices, and calculations.

Mission Control:

Mission Control is a feature that helps users manage open windows and virtual desktops (Spaces). It provides a bird's-eye view of all open applications and desktops for easy navigation and organization.

Launchpad:

Launchpad is an app launcher that displays a grid of app icons, similar to iOS. It provides a user-friendly way to access and organize installed applications.

Notification Center:

The Notification Center, accessible from the Menu Bar, displays notifications from various apps and system events. It also includes widgets for quick access to information like weather and calendar events.

Window Management:

macOS offers advanced window management features, including the ability to split the screen (Split View) between two apps, minimize windows to the Dock, and use full-screen mode for apps.

Universal Clipboard:

Universal Clipboard allows users to copy text, images, or files on one Apple device (e.g., iPhone or iPad) and paste them on their MacBook seamlessly, provided they are signed in to the same iCloud account.

Dark Mode:

macOS includes a Dark Mode, which changes the system interface and compatible apps to a darker color scheme, reducing eye strain in low-light environments.

Accessibility Features:

macOS offers a wide range of accessibility features, including VoiceOver (screen reader), Magnifier, closed captions, and more, to support users with disabilities.

Support: Gesture

macOS supports a variety of multi-touch gestures on the trackpad for tasks like scrolling, zooming, swiping between desktops, and navigating through web pages.

Keyboard Shortcuts:

macOS includes a robust set of keyboard shortcuts for efficient navigation and control. Users can create custom keyboard shortcuts for specific tasks.

Privacy Features:

macOS emphasizes user privacy and includes features like App Tracking Transparency and privacy reports that inform users about how apps access their data.

Security Features:

macOS includes security features like Gatekeeper (app verification), FileVault (disk encryption), and built-in antivirus protection to safeguard user data and privacy.

In summary, the macOS user interface is designed to provide an elegant, user-friendly, and highly functional computing experience on MacBook laptops and Mac desktops. Its features and customization options allow users to tailor their workspace and workflow to their preferences and needs, whether for productivity, creative tasks, or general use.

INSTALLING AND UPDATING MACOS

Installing and updating macOS is essential to keep your MacBook up to date with the latest features, improvements, and security patches. Here's a comprehensive explanation of how to install macOS and keep it up to date:

Installing macOS:
Check Compatibility:

Before installing macOS, ensure that your MacBook is compatible with the version of macOS you intend to install. Apple provides compatibility information on its official website.

Backup Your Data:

Before any major macOS installation, it's crucial to back up your data. You can use Time Machine or third-party backup solutions to create a full system backup.

Download macOS:

To install macOS, you'll need to download the installer from the Mac App Store or the Apple website. The installer is typically available for free.

Run the Installer:

Once the installer is downloaded, it will automatically open. If not, you can locate it in your Applications folder and double-click to run it.

Follow On-Screen Instructions:

The installer will guide you through the installation process. You'll need to agree to the terms and conditions, select the destination drive, and choose whether to perform a clean installation or upgrade from your existing macOS version.

Enter Your Apple ID:
You may be prompted to enter your Apple ID during the installation to link your Mac to your Apple services and apps.

Wait for Installation:
The installation process may take some time, and your MacBook will restart several times. Be patient and do not interrupt the process.

Set Up macOS:
After installation, you'll be guided through the initial setup, including selecting your region, language, creating a user account, and configuring system preferences.

Restore Data:
If you backed up your data, you can use Time Machine or other backup methods to restore your files and settings.

Updating macOS:
Check for Updates:
macOS updates are typically available through the "Software Update" feature in "System Preferences." You can also check for updates by clicking the Apple menu > "About This Mac" > "Software Update."

Download Updates:
When updates are available, you can download them directly from the "Software Update" menu. Your MacBook may notify you when updates are ready to install.

Install Updates:
Click "Install" to start the update process. Your MacBook will need to restart to complete some updates.

Automatic Updates:
You can enable automatic updates in "System Preferences" > "Software Update." This ensures that your MacBook always receives the latest updates automatically.

Tips for a Smooth Installation and Update Process:
Ensure that you have a stable internet connection during the download and installation processes.
Keep your MacBook plugged in or make sure it has sufficient battery charge to avoid interruptions during updates.
Backup your important data regularly to prevent data loss in case of unforeseen issues.
Check Apple's official website or support resources for any specific instructions or known issues related to the macOS version you are installing or updating.
Regularly installing macOS updates is crucial for keeping your MacBook secure, improving performance, and accessing the latest features. By following these steps and best practices, you can maintain a smooth and up-to-date macOS experience on your MacBook.

INITIAL SETUP

The initial setup of a MacBook involves configuring the operating system and personalizing the settings to suit your preferences. Here's a step-by-step guide on how to perform the initial setup for macOS:

Turning On the MacBook:
Press the power button on the MacBook to turn it on. The setup process will begin.

Select Your Language and Region:
Choose your preferred language and region.

Choose a Keyboard Layout:
Select the keyboard layout you'll be using. Typically, this is a standard keyboard layout for your region.

Choose Wi-Fi Network:
Connect to a Wi-Fi network to proceed with the setup. If you're not connected to the internet, some features may not be available during the setup.

Transfer Information to This Mac:
If you're upgrading from an old Mac or have a recent backup, you can choose to transfer your data, apps, and settings from another Mac or a Time Machine backup. Alternatively, you can choose to set up as a new Mac.

Sign in with Your Apple ID:
Sign in with your Apple ID. If you don't have an Apple ID, you can create one during this step.

Terms and Conditions:
Read and agree to the terms and conditions.

Create a Computer Account:
Create a username and password for your computer account. You can also set up a hint to help you remember your password.

iCloud Setup:
Choose whether to enable iCloud features such as iCloud Drive, Photos, Notes, and Find My Mac. You can customize these settings to your preference.

Enable Siri:
Choose whether to enable Siri, Apple's voice-activated assistant, during the setup process.

Diagnostics and Usage:
Choose whether to send diagnostic and usage data to Apple. This data helps Apple improve its products and services.

Set Up Touch ID (if applicable):

If your MacBook has Touch ID, you'll be prompted to set it up. Touch ID allows you to unlock your Mac and make secure purchases.

Create a Backup (optional):
Consider setting up Time Machine to create regular backups of your MacBook, ensuring your data is safe.

Choose a Theme (Light or Dark Mode):
macOS offers a choice between Light Mode and Dark Mode. Select your preferred theme.

Welcome to Your Mac:
Congratulations! You've completed the initial setup. Your Mac is now ready to use.

Additional Tips:
Familiarize yourself with the various settings and preferences in System Preferences to customize your Mac to your liking.
Explore the Mac App Store to discover and install applications that suit your needs.
Keep your MacBook updated with the latest macOS updates to ensure optimal performance and security.
By following these steps and customizing the settings to your preferences, you'll have a personalized and ready-to-use MacBook tailored to your needs and workflow.

SOFTWARE UPDATES

Software updates are essential for keeping your MacBook's operating system and installed applications up to date. They include bug fixes, performance improvements, new features, and security patches to enhance your device's functionality, stability, and security.

Here's a comprehensive explanation of software updates on macOS:

Types of Software Updates:
- **Operating System Updates:** These updates, often referred to as macOS updates, bring major changes and improvements to the core operating system. They may introduce new features, enhancements, and security updates.
- **App Updates:** Apps installed on your MacBook, including those from the Mac App Store and third-party sources, receive updates to fix bugs, improve performance, and add new features.

Why Software Updates Are Important:
- **Security:** Updates frequently include security patches to protect your MacBook from vulnerabilities and threats. It's crucial to keep your software up to date to prevent security breaches.

- **Stability:** Updates can fix software bugs and glitches that may cause crashes or unexpected behavior, improving the overall stability of your system.
- **Performance:** Updates often optimize system performance, making your MacBook run smoother and faster.
- **New Features:** Operating system updates may introduce new features and enhancements, enhancing your user experience.

How to Check for Updates:
macOS Updates:
Go to the Apple menu > "About This Mac."
Click on "Software Update" to check for available macOS updates.

App Updates:
For apps from the Mac App Store, open the App Store and click on "Updates" in the sidebar.
For apps from third-party sources, you may need to check for updates within each app or use the app developer's update mechanism.

Installing Updates:
macOS Updates:
Click "Update Now" to download and install available macOS updates.
You may need to restart your MacBook to complete the installation.

App Updates:
Click "Update" next to each app in the App Store to install app updates.
For third-party apps, follow the app developer's instructions for updating.

Automatic Updates:
You can enable automatic updates for macOS and apps in "System Preferences" > "Software Update." This ensures that your MacBook stays up to date without manual intervention.

Checking Update Status:
While macOS or apps are updating, you can check their progress in the "Software Update" or "App Store" sections, respectively.
Avoid interrupting updates or turning off your MacBook during the update process.

Uninstalling Problematic Updates:
In rare cases, an update may cause issues with your system or specific apps. You can uninstall problematic updates by following Apple's instructions or contacting Apple Support.

Keep Backups:
Before major macOS updates, it's a good practice to back up your data using Time Machine or other backup methods to ensure data safety.

System Integrity Protection (SIP):
macOS includes System Integrity Protection, a security feature that protects system files and directories. Be cautious when modifying or deleting system files, even if you encounter issues after an update.

Third-Party Software:
Some third-party apps may require updates to maintain compatibility with the latest macOS version. Check with app developers for compatibility information and updates.

In summary, regularly installing software updates is crucial for maintaining the security, stability, and performance of your MacBook. By keeping both the operating system and installed applications up to date, you can ensure that your MacBook functions smoothly and securely.

TROUBLESHOOTING MACOS ISSUES

Troubleshooting macOS issues is essential to keep your MacBook running smoothly and resolve any problems that may arise.

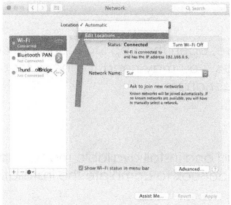

Here's a comprehensive guide on how to troubleshoot common macOS issues:

Identify the Problem:
Before troubleshooting, identify the specific issue you're facing. Is it related to performance, software, hardware, or connectivity?

Restart Your MacBook:
Sometimes, a simple restart can resolve minor issues. Click the Apple menu > "Restart" to reboot your MacBook.

Check for macOS Updates:
Ensure that your macOS is up to date. Go to the Apple menu > "About This Mac" > "Software Update" to check for and install any available updates.

Force Quit Unresponsive Apps:
If an application becomes unresponsive or freezes, you can force quit it by pressing "Command + Option + Esc" simultaneously. Select the app and click "Force Quit."

Clear Cache and Temporary Files:
Use macOS's built-in utility, "Disk Utility," to clear cache and temporary files. Open it, select your startup disk, and click "First Aid" > "Run."

Check Storage Space:
Insufficient storage space can slow down your MacBook. Free up space by deleting unnecessary files and apps.

MACBOOK GUIDE

Safe Boot:
Boot your MacBook into Safe Mode by restarting it and holding down the Shift key. This can help isolate and resolve issues caused by third-party software.

Reset NVRAM/PRAM:
Resetting the non-volatile RAM (NVRAM) or parameter RAM (PRAM) can resolve various hardware-related issues. Restart your MacBook and hold down "Command + Option + P + R" until you hear the startup chime twice.

Run Disk Utility:
Use Disk Utility to verify and repair disk errors. Open it, select your startup disk, and click "First Aid."

Check Activity Monitor:
Use the Activity Monitor app to identify resource-intensive processes or applications. You can force quit or troubleshoot any problematic ones.

Reset SMC (System Management Controller):
Resetting the SMC can help resolve hardware-related issues. The procedure varies depending on your MacBook's model, so refer to Apple's official guidelines for your specific model.

Create a New User Account:
If you suspect issues with your user account, create a new one and see if the problem persists. You can do this in "System Preferences" > "Users & Groups."

Check for Malware and Viruses:
While macOS is generally secure, it's not immune to malware. Use reputable antivirus and anti-malware software to scan your MacBook for threats.

Check Hardware Connections:
Ensure that all hardware components, such as external drives, monitors, and accessories, are properly connected.

Check Internet Connectivity:
If you're experiencing internet-related issues, check your Wi-Fi or Ethernet connection and router settings.

Visit the Apple Support Website:
Apple provides extensive support resources, including troubleshooting guides and forums, on its official website. You can search for solutions specific to your issue.

Consult Apple Support:
If you can't resolve the problem on your own, contact Apple Support or visit an Apple Store for professional assistance.

Backup Your Data:
Before attempting any major troubleshooting steps, ensure that you have a recent backup of your data using Time Machine or another backup method.

Remember that troubleshooting may require different approaches depending on the specific issue you're facing. If you're uncertain or uncomfortable with the troubleshooting process, it's advisable to seek professional assistance to avoid potential data loss or further complications.

COMMON PROBLEMS AND SOLUTIONS

Common problems on macOS can vary in their severity and impact on your workflow. Here's a comprehensive list of some typical issues and their respective solutions:

Slow Performance:
Solution:
Check available storage and free up space.
Close unnecessary apps and browser tabs.
Restart your MacBook to clear memory.
Run Disk Utility to check for disk errors and repair them.

Wi-Fi Connectivity Issues:
Solution:
Restart your MacBook and the router.
Forget and rejoin the Wi-Fi network.
Reset the network settings in "System Preferences" > "Network."
Check for interference and move closer to the router.

Battery Draining Quickly:
Solution:
Check for resource-intensive apps using Activity Monitor and close them.
Reduce screen brightness and use Energy Saver settings.
Reset SMC to recalibrate the battery.

MacBook Not Charging:
Solution:
Check the power cable and connections for damage.
Reset SMC to reset power management settings.
Visit an authorized service provider if the issue persists.

App Crashes or Freezes:
Solution:
Update the app to the latest version.
Restart your MacBook.
Check for macOS updates and install them.
Force quit the app using "Command + Option + Esc."

Bluetooth Connectivity Issues:
Solution:
Toggle Bluetooth off and on in "System Preferences."
Remove and re-pair Bluetooth devices.
Reset SMC to reset hardware settings.

Startup Disk Full:

Solution:

Delete unnecessary files and apps.

Empty the Trash to permanently delete files.

Use external storage or cloud services to offload data.

External Device Not Recognized:
Solution:

Check the connection and try a different port.

Restart your MacBook and try again.

Check the device on another computer to rule out hardware issues.

Display Issues:
Solution:

Check the display cables and connections.

Adjust display settings in "System Preferences."

Reset NVRAM/PRAM to reset display settings.

Spinning Beachball (System Hang):
Solution:

Check Activity Monitor to identify resource-hungry processes and close them.

Restart your MacBook to clear memory and processes.

Printer Problems:
Solution:

Ensure the printer is connected and turned on.

Update the printer driver from the manufacturer's website.

Reset the printing system in "System Preferences" > "Printers & Scanners."

MacBook Overheating:
Solution:

Check for resource-intensive apps and close them.

Use a laptop cooling pad.

Clean the MacBook's cooling vents.

Audio or Sound Issues:
Solution:

Check sound settings in "System Preferences" > "Sound."

Restart your MacBook.

Reset NVRAM/PRAM to reset audio settings.

File or App Permissions Issues:
Solution:

Check and adjust file permissions using "Get Info."

Reinstall the app to reset permissions.

Time Machine Backup Issues:
Solution:

Restart your MacBook and try the backup again.

Check for macOS updates and install them.
Reset Time Machine preferences if necessary.
For any critical or persistent issues, consider seeking assistance from Apple Support or an authorized service provider to ensure the problem is properly diagnosed and resolved.

USING maCOS RECOVERY OPTIONS

macOS recovery options provide essential tools and utilities for troubleshooting and repairing your MacBook in case of issues. There are several ways to access macOS recovery, each serving a specific purpose.

Here's a comprehensive explanation of using macOS recovery options:

Accessing macOS Recovery:
To access macOS recovery, follow these steps:
Restart your MacBook.
As it boots up, hold down the "Command + R" keys until you see the Apple logo or a spinning globe.
Release the keys to enter recovery mode.

macOS Utilities in Recovery Mode:
macOS recovery provides several utilities to help diagnose and fix issues:
Restore From Time Machine Backup:
If you have a Time Machine backup, you can use this option to restore your system to a previous state.

Reinstall macOS:
This option allows you to reinstall the current macOS version without losing your data. It's useful for repairing corrupted system files.
Disk Utility:
Disk Utility helps you manage and repair your storage devices, including internal and external drives. You can use it to verify and repair disk errors.

Get Help Online:
If you're facing internet-related issues, you can access Safari and browse the web for support resources while in recovery mode.

MACBOOK GUIDE

Using Disk Utility:
Disk Utility is a powerful tool for managing disks and volumes. Here's how to use it:
Select "Disk Utility" from the macOS Utilities menu.
Choose your startup disk and click "First Aid" to check and repair disk errors.
You can also use Disk Utility to format and partition drives if needed.

Reinstalling macOS:
If you need to reinstall macOS to address software-related issues, follow these steps:
Select "Reinstall macOS" from the macOS Utilities menu.
Follow the on-screen instructions to reinstall macOS while keeping your files and apps intact.

Restoring From Time Machine Backup:
If you have a Time Machine backup and want to restore your system to a previous state:
Select "Restore From Time Machine Backup" from the macOS Utilities menu.
Follow the on-screen instructions to select the backup date and initiate the restoration process.

Get Help Online:
To access Safari and browse the web for support resources:
Select "Get Help Online" from the macOS Utilities menu.
Connect to a Wi-Fi network and open Safari to search for solutions or visit Apple's support website.

Using Terminal in Recovery Mode:
If you're familiar with the Terminal, you can open it from the Utilities menu to perform advanced troubleshooting and administrative tasks.

Using Target Disk Mode:
If you have another Mac and a compatible cable, you can use Target Disk Mode to access the files on your MacBook's internal drive from another Mac.

Contacting Apple Support:
If you're unable to resolve the issue using the available tools, consider contacting Apple Support or visiting an Apple Store or authorized service provider for professional assistance.

Important Notes:
It's essential to back up your data regularly using Time Machine or another backup method to ensure that you can recover your files if needed.
Be cautious when using Disk Utility or Terminal, as making incorrect changes can lead to data loss.
Always ensure that your MacBook is connected to a stable power source or has sufficient battery charge when performing recovery operations.
In summary, macOS recovery options provide valuable tools for diagnosing and resolving issues with your

MacBook's operating system and storage. Understanding how to access and use these options can help you

troubleshoot and recover from various problems effectively.

4. MACBOOK PRODUCTIVITY

MacBook productivity refers to using your MacBook effectively and efficiently to accomplish tasks, work, and manage your digital life. MacBooks are known for their user-friendly design and powerful software, making them ideal tools for various productivity purposes. Here's a comprehensive explanation of MacBook productivity:

Operating System and Software:
- **macOS:** MacBooks run on macOS, which offers a stable, intuitive, and user-friendly interface for productivity tasks.

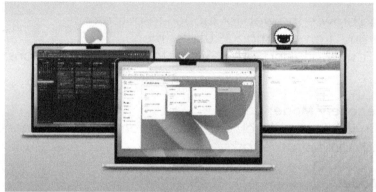

- **iWork Suite:** Apple's iWork suite includes Pages (word processing), Numbers (spreadsheet), and Keynote (presentation), making it easy to create documents, spreadsheets, and presentations.
- **Microsoft Office:** You can also install Microsoft Office apps (Word, Excel, PowerPoint) for compatibility with widely used productivity formats.
- **Third-Party Apps:** The Mac App Store offers a wide range of productivity apps, including project management tools, note-taking apps, and more.

Hardware Features for Productivity:
- **Retina Display:** High-resolution Retina displays provide sharp text and vibrant colors, reducing eye strain during long work sessions.

- **Backlit Keyboard:** Illuminated keyboards make typing in low-light conditions easier.
- **Trackpad Gestures:** Multi-touch trackpads support gestures for navigation, zooming, and scrolling.
- **Battery Life:** MacBooks offer long battery life, allowing for extended work sessions without constant charging.
- **Powerful CPUs:** MacBook models come with powerful processors for multitasking and handling resource-intensive tasks.

Productivity Software and Tools:
- **Productivity Suites:** Use software suites like Microsoft Office or iWork for document creation, spreadsheet management, and presentations.
- **Note-Taking Apps:** Apps like Apple Notes, Microsoft OneNote, or Evernote help you organize ideas, take notes, and sync them across devices.
- **Task and Project Management:** Tools like Todoist, Trello, or Asana assist in managing tasks and projects efficiently.
- **Email Clients:** Apps like Apple Mail, Microsoft Outlook, or third-party clients help manage email and appointments.
- **Cloud Storage:** Services like iCloud, Dropbox, Google Drive, or Microsoft OneDrive allow seamless file synchronization and collaboration.

Organization and Time Management:
- **Calendar:** Use the built-in Calendar app to schedule appointments, meetings, and reminders.
- **Contacts:** Organize your contacts and address book with the Contacts app.
- **Time Tracking:** Apps like Toggl or Clockify help track time spent on tasks and projects.
- **Focus and Pomodoro Techniques:** Apps like Focus@Will and Pomodone can improve focus and productivity.

Virtual Desktops and Multitasking:
macOS supports virtual desktops (Spaces) and Mission Control to manage multiple apps and tasks simultaneously.

Security and Privacy:
macOS includes robust security features, such as Gatekeeper and FileVault, to protect your data and privacy.

Communication and Collaboration:
- **Facetime:** Use FaceTime for video calls with colleagues and clients.
- **Messages:** The Messages app supports text, audio, and video communication.
- **Collaboration Tools:** Apps like Slack, Zoom, and Microsoft Teams enable team communication and collaboration.

Customization and Personalization:
macOS allows you to customize the desktop, dock, and system preferences to suit your workflow and preferences.

Automation and Scripting:
Automator and AppleScript enable users to automate repetitive tasks and create custom workflows.

Continuity Across Devices:
With Apple's ecosystem, you can seamlessly switch between your MacBook and other Apple devices like iPhone and iPad, sharing data and tasks.

Regular Updates:
macOS receives regular updates with performance enhancements, security fixes, and new features to improve productivity.

In summary, MacBook productivity encompasses a combination of hardware, software, tools, and techniques to help you efficiently complete tasks, manage your time, communicate effectively, and maintain a productive workflow. MacBooks are versatile devices suitable for a wide range of personal and professional productivity needs.

PRODUCTIVITY APPS

Productivity apps are software applications designed to help individuals and organizations streamline tasks, manage time, and accomplish goals more efficiently. These apps are available for various platforms, including macOS, and can enhance your productivity in different ways.

Project Management Apps:
- **Trello:** Trello uses boards, lists, and cards to help users manage projects, tasks, and workflows visually. It's excellent for collaborative work and tracking progress.
- **Asana:** Asana is a robust project management tool that offers task lists, timelines, and advanced project tracking features.
- **Microsoft Planner:** Part of the Microsoft 365 suite, Planner integrates with other Microsoft apps and provides a visual way to organize tasks.

Task Management Apps:
- **Todoist:** Todoist is a popular task manager that lets you create to-do lists, set deadlines, and organize tasks by projects and priorities.
- **Things:** Things is a sleek task manager for macOS and iOS that offers a clean interface and powerful task organization features.
- **Wunderlist (discontinued, replaced by Microsoft To Do):** Wunderlist was known for its simplicity and cross-platform compatibility, allowing users to create and manage to-do lists.

Note-Taking Apps:
- **Evernote:** Evernote is a versatile note-taking app that allows you to capture, organize, and sync notes, documents, images, and web clippings across devices.
- **Apple Notes:** Apple's native Notes app offers basic note-taking features, but it's user-friendly and integrates seamlessly with other Apple apps and devices.

- **Microsoft OneNote:** Part of the Microsoft 365 suite, OneNote is a robust note-taking app with advanced features like notebooks, sections, and tags.

Calendar and Scheduling Apps:
- **Apple Calendar:** The built-in Calendar app on macOS offers features for scheduling appointments, managing events, and setting reminders.
- **Microsoft Outlook:** Outlook is a powerful email client that also includes calendar and scheduling features, making it suitable for business use.

Time Management and Focus Apps:
- **Focus@Will:** Focus@Will plays background music scientifically designed to improve concentration and productivity.
- **Pomodone:** Pomodone uses the Pomodoro Technique to help users break work into intervals with timed breaks for improved focus.

Password Managers:
- **1Password:** 1Password stores and manages your passwords securely, making it easy to access websites and apps without memorizing complex passwords.
- **LastPass:** LastPass is another popular password manager that offers secure password storage and generation.

Cloud Storage and File Collaboration Apps:
- **Dropbox:** Dropbox allows you to store files in the cloud and share them with others. It integrates with macOS for seamless file management.
- **Google Drive:** Google Drive offers cloud storage and collaboration tools, including Google Docs, Sheets, and Slides, for real-time document editing.

Communication and Collaboration Apps:
- **Slack:** Slack is a team communication platform that streamlines internal messaging, file sharing, and integration with other productivity apps.
- **Microsoft Teams:** Part of the Microsoft 365 suite, Teams combines chat, video conferencing, and file sharing for efficient collaboration.

Automation and Scripting Apps:
- **Automator:** Built into macOS, Automator allows users to automate repetitive tasks by creating custom workflows.
- **AppleScript:** AppleScript is a scripting language for automating actions and tasks on macOS.

Finance and Expense Tracking Apps:
- **QuickBooks:** QuickBooks is accounting software for small businesses, helping with financial management, invoicing, and expense tracking.
- **YNAB (You Need a Budget):** YNAB is a budgeting app that helps users manage finances, track expenses, and save money.

These productivity apps cater to various needs, and the choice of app depends on your specific tasks and preferences. Incorporating these apps into your workflow can help you better manage time, stay organized, and improve overall productivity on your macOS device.

PRE-INSTALLED APPS (E.G., SAFARI, MAIL, CALENDAR)

Pre-installed apps, also known as default apps or built-in apps, are software applications that come pre-installed with the macOS operating system on your MacBook. These apps are designed to provide essential functionality and are an integral part of the macOS ecosystem.

Here's a comprehensive explanation of some of the commonly pre-installed apps on macOS:

Safari:
- **Purpose:** Safari is the default web browser for macOS. It allows users to browse the internet, access websites, and manage bookmarks.
- **Features:** Safari offers features like a reading list, tab management, private browsing, and integration with iCloud Keychain for password management.
- **Advantages:** It's known for its speed, energy efficiency, and privacy features, making it a reliable choice for web browsing on Mac.

Mail:
- **Purpose:** The Mail app is a versatile email client that allows users to manage multiple email accounts, send and receive emails, and organize messages.
- **Features:** Mail offers features like threaded conversations, smart mailboxes, and integration with Calendar and Contacts for scheduling and contact management.
- **Advantages:** It's an efficient email client with a clean user interface, making it easy to manage your email communication.

Opera:
Opera is a cross-platform web browser developed by the company of the same name, Opera. Additionally, mobile versions named Opera Mobile and Opera Mini exist. Opera users can also utilize Opera News, a news application powered by an AI platform.

Originally released on April 10, 1995, Opera stands as one of the oldest desktop web browsers that is still under active development. For its initial decade, it was commercial software and employed its own proprietary layout engine, Presto. In 2013, it transitioned from the Presto engine to Chromium. In 2016, Opera was purchased by an investment group led by a Chinese consortium.

The company unveiled a gaming-oriented version of the browser, Opera GX, in 2019, and a blockchain-focused Opera Crypto Browser in public beta in January 2022. In April 2023, the company announced a significant overhaul for the browser, named Opera 100 and code-named "Opera One", introducing a new user interface and several artificial intelligence-related features. Opera 100 was launched on June 20, 2023.

Opera introduced innovations that were later embraced by other web browsers, such as: Speed Dial, blocking of pop-ups, the ability to reopen recently closed tabs, incognito mode, and the concept of tabbed browsing.[58][59] It also offers a unique screenshot tool named Snapshot, which has image editing capabilities; along with in-built ad and tracking blockers.

Integrated Messaging Platforms

Within Opera's desktop version, users can directly access popular messaging apps like WhatsApp, Telegram, Facebook Messenger, Twitter, Instagram, TikTok, and VK.

Functionality and User-Friendliness

Opera provides a bookmark toolbar and a tool for managing downloads. The "Speed Dial" feature lets users save and view a myriad of webpage thumbnails when a new tab is launched.

Opera pioneered in supporting Cascading Style Sheets (CSS) as early as 1998.

The Opera Turbo function, which used to condense web pages (excluding HTTPS pages) before delivering them to users,has been removed from the desktop version but is still present in Opera Mini, their mobile browser version.

Safety and Confidentiality

Opera includes a feature to swiftly erase private information like HTTP cookies, browsing logs, cached items, and stored passwords.

When accessing a website, Opera showcases a security badge in the address bar, providing insights about the site, inclusive of its security credentials. Opera has an in-built system that alerts users about potentially harmful websites. This default feature cross-checks the accessed site with databases that list known phishing and malware-ridden websites, known as blacklists.

In 2016, Opera added a complimentary virtual private network (VPN) feature to the browser. his was claimed to facilitate encrypted browsing for blocked sites and assure safety on public WiFi connections. Later, it was clarified that this VPN functioned more like a web proxy, meaning it only encrypted browser-based activities and not actions by other computer applications.

Opera boasts numerous impressive functionalities, with its battery conservation technique standing out prominently. Based on Opera's evaluations, the browser's energy-efficient mode outlasts competitors like Google Chrome and Microsoft Edge by up to 35%. Depending on your laptop's model and specifications, this could translate to an additional hour of battery usage.

For smartphones and tablets, Opera optimizes web content to ensure speedy page loads, even on sluggish internet connections, reducing the waiting time for pages to appear.

The Opera internet browser effectively blocks pop-up advertisements. A significant feature that elevates the Opera browser is its integrated ad-blocking mechanism. This prevents ads from interrupting your browsing experience, leading to quicker page loads. The best part? This ad-blocker is built-in, with no need for extra plugins, downloads, or extensions, and it functions seamlessly on both desktop and mobile iterations.

Opera's own evaluations indicate that, with the ad blocker activated, content-heavy pages can load up to 90% more swiftly. However, if you wish, you can choose to allow ads on specific websites.

Opera offers seamless synchronization across all your gadgets. By setting up a complimentary Opera account, which comes with its own Opera email, you can ensure consistent browsing data across all your devices. Simply log in to every device, and your frequently visited site shortcuts, bookmarks, and current open tabs will harmonize across all platforms.

Opera's unique feature, Flow, bridges the Opera browser on PCs with Opera Touch on mobiles, centralizing videos, links, images, and notes. Flow is straightforward – there's no need for account setups or passwords. Just scan the provided QR code from your PC to your smartphone.

Calendar:
- **Purpose:** Calendar is a scheduling app that helps users manage events, appointments, and tasks. It integrates with iCloud and other calendar services.
- **Features:** Users can create events, set reminders, send invitations, and view calendars in various formats, including day, week, month, and year.
- **Advantages:** Calendar simplifies time management and provides a unified view of upcoming events and appointments.

Notes:
- **Purpose:** The Notes app allows users to create and organize notes, checklists, and sketches. It syncs across Apple devices using iCloud.
- **Features:** Notes supports formatting options, attachments, and the ability to categorize notes into folders.
- **Advantages:** It's a versatile note-taking app for jotting down ideas, making to-do lists, and storing important information.

Reminders:
- **Purpose:** Reminders is a task management app that helps users create and organize to-do lists and reminders.
- **Features:** Users can set due dates, locations, and priority levels for tasks. Reminders syncs across Apple devices and supports natural language input.
- **Advantages:** It's a handy app for managing tasks and staying organized, and it integrates with Calendar and Siri.

Maps:
- **Purpose:** Maps is a navigation and mapping app that provides directions, points of interest, and real-time traffic information.
- **Features:** Users can get driving, walking, and transit directions, view 3D maps, and access detailed location information.
- **Advantages:** Maps is a useful app for planning routes, finding nearby businesses, and exploring new places.

Photos:
- **Purpose:** Photos is a multimedia management app for organizing and editing photos and videos.
- **Features:** It offers tools for creating albums, organizing media by date and location, and making basic edits like cropping and enhancing photos.
- **Advantages:** Photos simplifies the management and editing of your media library and syncs with iCloud for easy access across devices.

Messages:
- **Purpose:** Messages is a messaging app for sending and receiving text messages, photos, videos, and audio messages.
- **Features:** Users can engage in one-on-one or group chats, send stickers, use iMessage effects, and sync messages across Apple devices.
- **Advantages:** Messages is an intuitive app for staying in touch with friends and family, and it offers end-to-end encryption for security.

These pre-installed apps are designed to provide essential functionality for common tasks and activities on your MacBook. They are integrated into the macOS ecosystem, ensuring a seamless user experience and compatibility with other Apple devices and services. While you can use third-party apps for similar purposes, these default apps serve as a solid foundation for productivity and everyday use.

THIRD-PARTY PRODUCTIVITY APPS

Third-party productivity apps are software applications developed by companies or individuals other than the operating system's manufacturer (in the case of macOS, Apple). These apps offer a wide range of features and functionalities to enhance productivity, organization, and efficiency. Here's a comprehensive explanation of third-party productivity apps for macOS:

Task and Project Management:
- **Todoist:** Todoist is a popular task manager that helps you create to-do lists, set deadlines, and organize tasks by projects and priorities. It offers a clean and intuitive interface.
- **Asana:** Asana is a comprehensive project management tool that enables teams to plan, track, and manage projects, tasks, and workflows. It's suitable for both individual and collaborative work.
- **Trello:** Trello uses boards, lists, and cards to help users manage projects, tasks, and workflows visually. It's known for its simplicity and ease of use.

Note-Taking and Organization:
- **Evernote:** Evernote is a versatile note-taking app that allows you to capture, organize, and sync notes, documents, images, and web clippings across devices. It offers advanced search and organization features.
- **Notion:** Notion is an all-in-one workspace that combines note-taking, task management, databases, and collaboration tools. It's highly customizable and suitable for various use cases.
- **Bear:** Bear is a minimalistic note-taking app that offers a distraction-free writing environment. It supports markdown, tags, and organization features.

File Management and Cloud Storage:
- **Dropbox:** Dropbox is a cloud storage and file synchronization service that allows you to store, access, and share files across devices. It integrates seamlessly with macOS.
- **Google Drive:** Google Drive offers cloud storage and collaboration tools, including Google Docs, Sheets, and Slides, for real-time document editing and sharing.
- **OneDrive:** Microsoft's OneDrive provides cloud storage and integrates with Microsoft 365 apps for document editing and collaboration.

Email Clients:
- **Spark:** Spark is a feature-rich email client for macOS that offers smart inbox management, email scheduling, and collaboration features for teams.
- **Airmail:** Airmail is a customizable email client with advanced features like snooze, integration with various third-party apps, and support for multiple email accounts.
- **Mailbird:** Mailbird is an email client that focuses on simplicity and productivity, with features like unified inboxes and integrations with productivity apps.

Time Management and Focus Apps:
- **Focus@Will:** Focus@Will plays background music scientifically designed to improve concentration and productivity.
- **Pomodone:** Pomodone uses the Pomodoro Technique to help users break work into intervals with timed breaks for improved focus.
- **RescueTime:** RescueTime tracks your computer usage to help you understand how you spend your time and improve productivity.

Communication and Collaboration:
- **Slack:** Slack is a team communication platform that streamlines internal messaging, file sharing, and integration with productivity apps.
- **Microsoft Teams:** Microsoft Teams combines chat, video conferencing, and file sharing for efficient collaboration within organizations.
- **Zoom:** Zoom is a popular video conferencing and web meeting platform for virtual meetings and webinars.

Password Managers:
- 1Password: 1Password stores and manages your passwords securely, making it easy to access websites and apps without memorizing complex passwords.
- LastPass: LastPass is another popular password manager that offers secure password storage and generation.

Finance and Expense Tracking Apps:
- **QuickBooks:** QuickBooks is accounting software for small businesses, helping with financial management, invoicing, and expense tracking.
- **YNAB (You Need a Budget):** YNAB is a budgeting app that helps users manage finances, track expenses, and save money.

These third-party productivity apps for macOS offer diverse features and cater to different needs. Users can customize their productivity toolkit by selecting the apps that best align with their preferences and workflow requirements. Many of these apps also offer cross-platform compatibility, allowing users to access their productivity tools on multiple devices.

ORGANIZING AND MANAGING FILES

Organizing and managing files is a crucial aspect of maintaining productivity and keeping your digital workspace efficient and clutter-free. On macOS, you can utilize various built-in features and third-party applications to help you organize and manage your files effectively.

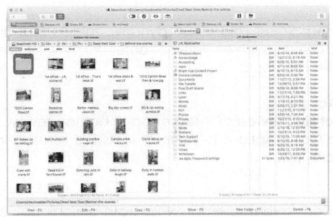

Here's a comprehensive guide on organizing and managing files on your MacBook:

Use the Finder:
Finder is macOS's built-in file management tool. It provides a visual interface to navigate, organize, and search for files and folders.

File Hierarchy:
Create a clear and organized file hierarchy: Organize your files and folders into a logical structure. For example, you can have top-level folders for work, personal, and project-related files. Within these folders, create subfolders for further organization.

File Naming Conventions:
- **Adopt consistent file naming conventions:** Use clear and descriptive names for files and folders. Include dates, project names, and relevant keywords in file names to make them easy to locate.

Use Tags and Labels:
- **macOS allows you to tag files and folders:** Tags help you categorize and locate items quickly. You can create custom tags based on your organization needs, such as "Work," "Personal," or "Urgent."

Spotlight Search:
- **Leverage Spotlight Search:** Press "Command + Space" to open Spotlight. This powerful search tool can quickly locate files, folders, apps, and even perform calculations or web searches.

Stacks:
- **Enable Stacks:** Stacks automatically organize files on your desktop into neat stacks based on file type or tags. Right-click on the desktop and choose "Use Stacks" to enable this feature.

iCloud Drive:
- **Utilize iCloud Drive:** iCloud Drive stores your files in the cloud, making them accessible on all your Apple devices. It helps you keep your files synchronized and organized across platforms.

Smart Folders:
- **Create Smart Folders:** Smart Folders are dynamic folders that automatically collect files based on specific criteria, such as file type, date, or keyword. They can save you time by keeping related files together.

File Preview and Quick Actions:
- **Take advantage of file previews:** Press the space bar to preview a file without opening it. You can also use Quick Actions to perform tasks like rotating images or creating PDFs directly from the preview.

Empty Trash Regularly:
- **Empty the Trash:** Don't forget to empty your Trash periodically to free up space on your hard drive.

Time Machine Backup:
- **Back up your files:** Use Time Machine to automatically back up your files. This ensures you can recover data in case of accidental deletions or hardware failures.

Third-Party File Managers:
- **Consider third-party file managers:** Apps like Pathfinder or Forklift offer advanced file management features, including dual-pane navigation and enhanced file operations.

Cloud-Based Storage Services:
- **Use cloud-based storage services:** Services like Dropbox, Google Drive, and OneDrive provide seamless file synchronization and backup capabilities. They also offer mobile access to your files.

Duplicate File Finder:
- **Run a duplicate file finder:** Use apps like Gemini or Duplicate Detective to identify and remove duplicate files, freeing up storage space.

Batch Renaming:
- **Batch rename files:** If you have a large number of files with inconsistent names, consider using batch renaming tools to bring uniformity to your file naming conventions.

File Encryption:
- **Consider file encryption:** If you need to secure sensitive files, use macOS's built-in FileVault or third-party encryption software to protect your data.

Regular Maintenance:
- **Perform regular maintenance:** Clean up your files and folders periodically to remove outdated or unnecessary items. This helps maintain a clutter-free environment.

By implementing these file organization and management strategies, you can maintain a tidy and efficient digital workspace on your MacBook, making it easier to find, access, and work with your files effectively.

FINDER TIPS AND TRICKS

Finder is the built-in file management tool on macOS, and it offers a range of tips and tricks to help you navigate and manage your files more efficiently. Here's a comprehensive list of Finder tips and tricks to enhance your file management experience on your MacBook:

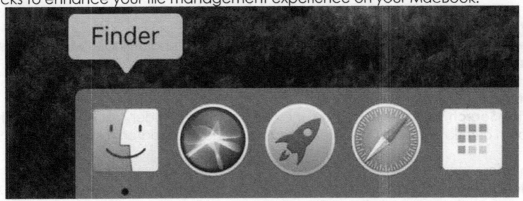

Keyboard Shortcuts:
- **Use keyboard shortcuts:** Learn essential keyboard shortcuts for Finder, such as "Command + N" for opening a new Finder window, "Command + C" for copying files, and "Command + V" for pasting files.

Quick Look:
- **Quick Look:** Select a file and press the space bar to preview it instantly. You can view documents, images, and even play videos without opening any apps.

Column View:
- **Use Column View:** In Finder, choose "View" > "as Columns." This view is especially useful for navigating deep folder structures, as it displays the hierarchy clearly.

Split View:
- **Split View:** To view two folders side by side, click and hold the green "Full-Screen" button in the top-left corner of a Finder window, and then select "Tile Window to Left of Screen" or "Tile Window to Right of Screen."

Sidebar Customization:
- **Customize the Sidebar:** Drag and drop folders and locations into the Finder sidebar for quick access. Right-click on the sidebar to hide or show specific items.

Favorites:
- **Add items to Favorites:** Drag frequently used folders to the Favorites section in the sidebar for easy access. You can also use the "Add to Favorites" option in the right-click menu.

Tags:
- **Use Tags:** Assign tags to files and folders by right-clicking and selecting "Tags." Tags help you categorize and locate items quickly.

Preview Pane:
- **Enable the Preview Pane:** Click the "View" menu and select "Show Preview" to display a preview of the selected file in the right-hand pane of the Finder window.

Smart Folders:
- **Create Smart Folders:** Smart Folders automatically collect files based on specific criteria. You can create them by clicking "File" > "New Smart Folder."

Tabbed Windows:
- **Use Tabbed Windows:** To keep multiple folders in a single Finder window, use tabs. You can open a new tab by pressing "Command + T" or clicking "File" > "New Tab."

Search Filters:
- **Utilize Search Filters:** When using the search bar in Finder, click the "+" button to add search criteria like file type, date, or tags to refine your search results.

Batch Rename:
- **Batch Rename Files:** Select multiple files, right-click, and choose "Rename X Items" to apply a batch renaming format.

Instant File Deletion:
- **Instantly Delete Files:** To skip moving files to the Trash, press "Option + Command + Delete" after selecting the files.

Custom Icon View:
- **Custom Icon View:** In Icon View, you can adjust the icon size and spacing by right-clicking in an empty area and selecting "Show View Options."

Quick Actions:
- **Use Quick Actions:** In the Preview pane, you'll find Quick Actions that allow you to perform tasks like rotating images or creating PDFs.

Automator Workflows:
- **Create Automator Workflows:** Automator can help you automate repetitive tasks in Finder. Create custom workflows to streamline file management processes.

Drag and Drop:
- **Drag and Drop:** You can drag files directly from Finder into applications like Mail, Messages, or other apps that support file attachment.

Copy Path:
- **Copy File Path:** Hold "Option" while right-clicking a file to copy its full file path. This is helpful when you need to reference or share a specific file location.

Force Quit Finder:
- **Force Quit Finder:** If Finder becomes unresponsive, you can force quit it by pressing "Option + Command + Escape" and selecting Finder from the list.

Integration with iCloud:
- **Use iCloud Drive:** If you use iCloud, your files are accessible across all your Apple devices. You can access your iCloud Drive from Finder.

By mastering these Finder tips and tricks, you'll be able to navigate, organize, and manage your files on your MacBook more efficiently, making your daily computing tasks smoother and more productive.

CLOUD STORAGE OPTIONS (E.G., ICLOUD, DROPBOX)

Cloud storage services offer convenient and secure ways to store, access, and share your files and data over the internet. They have become an integral part of modern digital life, allowing users to access their files from various devices and collaborate with others.

Here's a comprehensive explanation of some popular cloud storage options, including iCloud and Dropbox:

iCloud:
- **Provider:** Apple Inc.
- **Integration:** iCloud is tightly integrated with the Apple ecosystem, making it the default cloud storage for macOS, iOS, and other Apple devices.
- **Storage Options:** iCloud offers various storage plans, including 5 GB of free storage for every Apple ID. Paid plans range from 50 GB to 2 TB.

Features:
- **File Storage:** iCloud stores photos, videos, documents, app data, and more.
- **Automatic Backup:** It automatically backs up your iOS device, including photos, app data, settings, and more.
- **Sync Across Devices:** iCloud syncs your contacts, calendars, reminders, notes, and Safari bookmarks across all your Apple devices.
- **Collaboration:** You can collaborate on documents using iCloud Drive and the iWork suite (Pages, Numbers, Keynote).
- **Security:** iCloud features strong encryption and two-factor authentication for data protection.
- **Cross-Platform Access:** While primarily designed for Apple devices, iCloud can also be accessed from a web browser on Windows and Android devices.

Dropbox:
- **Provider:** Dropbox, Inc.
- **Integration:** Dropbox is a platform-independent cloud storage service available on macOS, Windows, Linux, iOS, Android, and via web browsers.
- **Storage Options:** Dropbox offers a free basic plan with 2 GB of storage. Paid plans provide more storage, ranging from 2 TB to unlimited storage for businesses.

Features:

- **File and Folder Sync:** Dropbox synchronizes files and folders across devices, allowing easy access from anywhere.
- **File Sharing:** You can share files and folders with others, including the ability to set permissions (view-only, edit) and create shared links.
- **Collaboration:** Dropbox Paper allows real-time document collaboration.
- **Automatic Camera Upload:** Automatically back up photos and videos from your mobile devices.
- **Security:** Dropbox uses encryption in transit and at rest, and it offers two-factor authentication for added security.
- **Cross-Platform Access:** It supports a wide range of operating systems and devices, making it suitable for both personal and business use.

Google Drive:
- **Provider:** Google LLC
- **Integration:** Google Drive is deeply integrated with Google's suite of productivity apps, such as Google Docs, Sheets, and Slides, and is available on macOS, Windows, iOS, Android, and the web.
- **Storage Options:** Google Drive offers 15 GB of free storage with options for additional storage through paid plans, starting at 100 GB.

Features:
- **Office Suite Integration:** Google Drive includes Google Workspace (formerly G Suite), allowing real-time collaboration on documents, spreadsheets, and presentations.
- **File Sharing:** You can easily share files and folders, set permissions, and create shareable links.
- **Search:** Google's powerful search engine is integrated into Google Drive, making it easy to find files.
- **Offline Access:** You can enable offline access to your Google Drive files for when you're not connected to the internet.
- Security: Google Drive uses encryption in transit and at rest, and it offers two-factor authentication for account protection.
- **Cross-Platform Access:** Google Drive is accessible from various devices and platforms.

Microsoft OneDrive:
- **Provider:** Microsoft Corporation
- **Integration:** OneDrive is tightly integrated with the Microsoft ecosystem, including Windows, macOS, iOS, and Android.
- **Storage Options:** OneDrive offers 5 GB of free storage with additional storage available through Microsoft 365 (formerly Office 365) subscriptions, starting at 1 TB.

Features:
- **Office Suite Integration:** OneDrive integrates seamlessly with Microsoft 365 apps, facilitating collaboration on Word, Excel, and PowerPoint documents.
- **File Sharing:** You can share files and folders with others, set permissions, and collaborate on documents in real-time.
- **Automatic Camera Upload:** Back up photos and videos from your mobile devices automatically.

- **Security:** OneDrive uses encryption in transit and at rest and offers two-factor authentication to protect your data.
- **Cross-Platform Access:** It's accessible from various devices and platforms, including Windows, macOS, iOS, and Android.

Choosing the right cloud storage option depends on your specific needs, device ecosystem, and the level of integration and collaboration features you require. These services offer various storage plans and features to cater to both personal and business use cases, ensuring your files are accessible and secure no matter where you are.

MULTITASKING AND GESTURES

Multitasking and gestures are essential features in macOS that enhance your productivity and make it easier to navigate and manage multiple tasks on your MacBook.

These features allow you to switch between apps, organize windows, and perform various actions using intuitive touchpad gestures.

Here's a comprehensive explanation of multitasking and gestures in macOS:

Multitasking:
Mission Control:
- **Purpose:** Mission Control provides an overview of all open windows, spaces, and full-screen apps, helping you manage and navigate between them.
- **Activation:** You can activate Mission Control by swiping up with three or four fingers on your trackpad, pressing the F3 key (or Control + Up Arrow), or using a gesture like a three-finger swipe up.
- **Usage:** In Mission Control, you can create new desktop spaces, drag and drop apps to different spaces, and select the window you want to focus on.

Spaces:
- **Purpose:** Spaces allow you to create virtual desktops, each with its own set of open apps and windows. It helps you organize your work into different contexts.
- **Activation:** You can switch between spaces using Mission Control or by swiping left or right with three or four fingers on the trackpad.
- **Usage:** Spaces are particularly useful for organizing different projects or separating work from personal tasks. You can move apps between spaces and customize the arrangement.

Full-Screen Apps:
- **Purpose:** Many apps on macOS support full-screen mode, which maximizes the app window to fill the entire screen, reducing distractions.

- **Activation:** Click the green "Full-Screen" button in the top-left corner of a compatible app's window or use the swipe-up gesture with three or four fingers to enter full-screen mode.
- **Usage:** Full-screen apps are great for focused work or when you want to dedicate your entire screen to a specific task. You can switch between full-screen apps using Mission Control or gestures.

App Exposé:

- **Purpose:** App Exposé displays all open windows for the current app, making it easy to switch between different documents or browser tabs within the same app.
- **Activation:** Click and hold on an app's icon in the Dock, or use the three-finger swipe down gesture on the trackpad while the cursor is over the app's icon.
- **Usage:** App Exposé helps you find and switch to the specific window you need when an app has multiple open windows.

Gestures:
Trackpad Gestures:

- **Swipe Gestures:** You can use swipe gestures on the trackpad to perform various actions. For example:
- Swipe left or right with two fingers to navigate web pages or documents.
- Pinch with two fingers to zoom in and out on images and web pages.
- Swipe up or down with two fingers to scroll through content.
- **Three-Finger Gestures:** Three-finger gestures are especially useful for multitasking and navigation:
- Swipe up with three fingers to access Mission Control.
- Swipe left or right with three fingers to switch between spaces.
- Swipe down with three fingers to activate App Exposé for the current app.

Hot Corners:

- **Purpose:** Hot Corners allow you to assign actions to specific corners of your screen, such as activating Mission Control or putting the display to sleep.
- **Configuration:** You can configure Hot Corners in System Preferences > Mission Control.
- **Usage:** Hover your cursor over a designated corner to trigger the assigned action.

Swipe Between Full-Screen Apps:

- **Purpose:** You can swipe between full-screen apps using a three-finger left or right swipe gesture on the trackpad.
- **Usage:** This is a convenient way to switch between full-screen apps without exiting full-screen mode.

Zoom Gesture:

- **Purpose:** You can enable zoom gestures in Accessibility settings, allowing you to zoom in on the entire screen or specific areas using various trackpad gestures.
- **Usage:** Useful for users with visual impairments or for magnifying specific content.

Gestures and multitasking features in macOS offer an intuitive and efficient way to interact with your MacBook, helping you navigate between apps, organize your workspace, and perform various actions with ease. Understanding and mastering these gestures can significantly improve your productivity and overall user experience on your MacBook.

MACBOOK SECURITY

MacBook security is a crucial aspect of using Apple's laptop computers, like the MacBook Air and MacBook Pro, to protect your data, privacy, and the overall integrity of your system. Here's an explanation of some key elements of MacBook security:

Operating System Security:
- **macOS:** The operating system running on MacBooks is called macOS. Apple regularly releases security updates and patches for macOS to address vulnerabilities and threats. It's important to keep your system up to date by enabling automatic updates.

User Accounts and Passwords:
- Always set a strong password for your user account. A strong password should be complex, containing a mix of uppercase and lowercase letters, numbers, and symbols.
- Consider using Touch ID or Face ID (if available) for quick and secure access to your MacBook.

FileVault Encryption:
- FileVault is a built-in disk encryption feature in macOS. It encrypts the entire startup disk, protecting your data from unauthorized access even if someone gains physical access to your MacBook.

Firewall:
- macOS includes a firewall that can be configured to block incoming network connections. You can enable it to add an extra layer of protection.

Gatekeeper:
- Gatekeeper is a security feature that helps protect your Mac from downloading and installing malicious software. It ensures that only apps from the App Store or identified

developers are allowed to run by default. You can adjust these settings in System Preferences.

App Store Security:
- Apps downloaded from the official Mac App Store are generally vetted and considered safer. However, it's essential to review app permissions and reviews before downloading any software.

Antivirus Software:
- While macOS has built-in security features, some users opt for third-party antivirus software to provide an additional layer of protection against malware and viruses.

Two-Factor Authentication (2FA):
- Enable two-factor authentication for your Apple ID and other online accounts associated with your MacBook. This adds an extra layer of security by requiring a second verification step, such as a code sent to your mobile device, when logging in.

Secure Browsing and Email:
- Use secure and updated web browsers and email clients. Be cautious of phishing emails and suspicious websites.

Regular Backups:
- Regularly back up your data using Time Machine or other backup solutions. In case of data loss or a security incident, having a recent backup ensures you can recover your files.

Privacy Settings:
- Review and adjust privacy settings in macOS to control which apps and services have access to your personal information, location, and other sensitive data.

Physical Security:
- Don't leave your MacBook unattended in public places. Consider using a cable lock or a secure bag when traveling.

Remote Management:
- Use "Find My Mac" to locate and remotely erase your MacBook in case it's lost or stolen. This feature also allows you to lock your device and display a custom message on the screen.

Secure Wi-Fi and Networking:

- Connect to trusted Wi-Fi networks and avoid open or public networks without proper security. Use a VPN for additional privacy and security when browsing on public networks.

Security Updates:
- Always install the latest security updates and patches provided by Apple promptly.

By following these security practices and staying vigilant, you can help ensure that your MacBook and your data remain safe from various threats and vulnerabilities. Remember that security is an ongoing process, and it's essential to stay informed about new threats and best practices.

SECURITY FEATURES

Security features are mechanisms, tools, or practices designed to protect computer systems, data, and networks from unauthorized access, data breaches, malware, and other potential threats. These features are essential in maintaining the confidentiality, integrity, and availability of digital assets. Here's an explanation of some common security features:

Authentication:
- Authentication is the process of verifying the identity of a user or system before granting access. Common methods include passwords, biometrics (e.g., fingerprint or facial recognition), smart cards, and two-factor authentication (2FA).

Authorization:
- Authorization determines what actions and resources a user or system is allowed to access after successful authentication. Access control lists (ACLs) and role-based access control (RBAC) are commonly used authorization mechanisms.

Encryption:
- Encryption transforms data into an unreadable format, and only authorized parties with the decryption key can access the original data. It's used to protect data at rest (on storage devices) and in transit (during communication over networks).

Firewalls:
- Firewalls are network security devices that filter incoming and outgoing network traffic. They can block or allow traffic based on predefined rules, protecting a network from unauthorized access and threats.

Intrusion Detection and Prevention Systems (IDPS):
- IDPS monitor network or system activities for signs of malicious behavior or policy violations. They can alert administrators or take automated actions to mitigate threats.

Antivirus and Antimalware Software:
- These programs scan for and remove malicious software, such as viruses, worms, Trojans, and spyware, to prevent them from infecting a system.

Security Updates and Patch Management:
- Regularly applying security updates and patches for operating systems, applications, and firmware helps close known vulnerabilities that hackers can exploit.

Security Auditing and Logging:
- Logging captures records of system and network activities, which can be used for security monitoring, incident investigation, and compliance purposes.

Virtual Private Networks (VPNs):
- VPNs create secure, encrypted tunnels over public networks (like the internet) to protect data transmitted between remote locations or devices.

Biometrics:
- Biometric authentication uses unique physical or behavioral traits, such as fingerprints, facial recognition, or voice patterns, to verify a person's identity.

Secure Boot and Firmware Integrity:
- Secure Boot ensures that only trusted and verified firmware, drivers, and operating system components are loaded during system startup, preventing the installation of malicious code at boot time.

Data Loss Prevention (DLP):
- DLP solutions prevent the unauthorized sharing or leakage of sensitive data by monitoring and controlling data transfers, even through email or cloud services.

Network Segmentation:
- Network segmentation divides a network into smaller, isolated segments to limit lateral movement of threats, containing potential breaches.

Multi-Factor Authentication (MFA):
- MFA requires users to provide two or more separate authentication factors (e.g., something you know, something you have, something you are) to access an account or system, making it harder for unauthorized users to gain access.

Backup and Disaster Recovery:
- Regularly backing up data and having a disaster recovery plan in place ensures that critical data can be restored in case of data loss or system failure.

User Education and Training:
- Security awareness training helps users recognize and respond to security threats, reducing the likelihood of falling victim to phishing, social engineering, or other attacks.

Security Policies and Compliance:
- Establishing security policies and adhering to industry-specific compliance standards (e.g., GDPR, HIPAA) helps organizations maintain a structured approach to security.

These security features are often used in combination to create a robust defense against various cyber threats. The specific security measures you need will depend on your organization's risk profile, the nature of your data, and your technology environment. It's essential to regularly assess and update your security posture to adapt to evolving threats.

<u>ONLINE SECURITY</u>

MacBook online security refers to the measures and practices you can employ to protect your MacBook and your personal information while connected to the internet. With the increasing prevalence of online threats and cyberattacks, maintaining robust online security is essential. Here's an explanation of key aspects of MacBook online security:

Secure Browsing:
- Use a secure web browser, like Safari, and ensure it's up to date. Browsers often receive security updates that address vulnerabilities.
- Look for the padlock symbol in the address bar, indicating a secure connection (https://) when visiting websites, especially when entering sensitive information.

Phishing Awareness:
- Be cautious of emails, messages, or websites that ask for personal information, login credentials, or financial details. Verify the sender's legitimacy before responding or clicking on links.
- Use email filters and spam detectors to help identify phishing attempts.

Strong Passwords:
Create strong, unique passwords for your online accounts, including your Apple ID. Consider using a password manager to generate and store complex passwords securely.

Two-Factor Authentication (2FA):
- Enable 2FA for your Apple ID and other online accounts when available. It adds an extra layer of security by requiring a second verification step, typically a code sent to your mobile device.

Secure Wi-Fi Connection:
- Connect to trusted Wi-Fi networks, and avoid using open or public networks without proper security. Public Wi-Fi networks are often less secure and can be targeted by hackers.
- Use a VPN (Virtual Private Network) when connecting to public networks to encrypt your internet traffic and protect your data from eavesdropping.

Firewall:
- Enable the built-in firewall on your MacBook. It helps block unauthorized incoming connections and provides an added layer of security.

Software Updates:
- Regularly update your MacBook's operating system, browsers, and software applications. Security patches are often included in these updates to fix vulnerabilities.

Email Security:
- Use an email client with built-in security features. Be cautious of email attachments and links, as they can be used to spread malware.
- Avoid clicking on suspicious email links, and don't download attachments from unknown sources.

Secure File Sharing:
- Use secure file-sharing methods, such as encrypted email or cloud storage services with strong security features, when sharing sensitive documents.

Secure Online Transactions:
- When making online purchases or financial transactions, ensure that the website uses secure connections (https://) and consider using trusted payment methods like Apple Pay.

Safe Download Practices:
- Only download software and apps from trusted sources, such as the Mac App Store or official websites of reputable developers. Be cautious of pirated or cracked software.

Privacy Settings:
- Review and adjust privacy settings on your MacBook to control which apps and services have access to your personal information, location, and other sensitive data.

Online Account Security:
- Periodically review and secure your online accounts by changing passwords, enabling security features, and monitoring account activity.

Backups:
- Regularly back up your data using Time Machine or cloud-based backup services. This ensures that you can recover your data in case of a security incident.

Security Education:
- Stay informed about the latest online security threats and best practices. Educate yourself about common scams and cyberattack techniques.
- By implementing these online security measures, you can significantly reduce the risk of falling victim to online threats and ensure the safety of your MacBook and your personal data while connected to the internet.

INTERNET SAFETY AND PRIVACY

Internet safety and privacy are vital aspects of maintaining your security and protecting your personal information while using the internet. Here's an explanation of these concepts and some key practices to ensure your online safety and privacy:

Internet Safety:
Internet safety refers to the measures and practices individuals take to protect themselves from online threats and risks, including cyberattacks, scams, identity theft, and exposure to harmful content. Here are some important aspects of internet safety:

- **Secure Passwords**: Create strong and unique passwords for your online accounts. Use a combination of letters, numbers, and symbols, and avoid easily guessable information like birthdays or names.
- **Two-Factor Authentication (2FA):** Enable 2FA whenever possible for your online accounts. It adds an extra layer of security by requiring you to provide a secondary verification method, such as a code sent to your phone.
- **Browsing Safety:** Use secure web browsers and keep them updated. Be cautious of suspicious websites and links, and avoid downloading files from untrustworthy sources.
- **Email Security:** Be wary of phishing emails and spam. Don't click on links or download attachments from unknown senders, and verify the legitimacy of requests for personal or financial information.
- **Privacy Settings:** Review and adjust the privacy settings on your social media accounts and other online services. Limit the amount of personal information you share publicly.
- **Safe Online Transactions:** When making online purchases, ensure that the website uses secure connections (https://) and use trusted payment methods. Be cautious of online sellers who ask for unusual payment methods.
- **Antivirus and Antimalware:** Install reputable antivirus and antimalware software to protect your devices from viruses, malware, and other threats.
- **Wi-Fi Security:** Use secure Wi-Fi networks, avoid public or unsecured networks, and consider using a VPN for additional security when connecting to public Wi-Fi.
- **Social Media Awareness:** Be mindful of what you share on social media. Oversharing personal information can make you a target for cybercriminals.

Internet Privacy:
Internet privacy concerns the protection of your personal data and online activities from unauthorized access, tracking, or misuse. Here are some key aspects of internet privacy:
- **Data Encryption:** Use encrypted communication methods, such as HTTPS websites and secure messaging apps, to protect your data while it's transmitted over the internet.
- **Virtual Private Network (VPN):** A VPN can help mask your IP address and encrypt your internet traffic, enhancing your privacy online.

- **Browser Privacy:** Configure your web browser to block third-party cookies and tracking mechanisms. Consider using privacy-focused browsers like Mozilla Firefox or extensions like Privacy Badger.
- **Privacy Tools:** Use privacy-focused search engines like DuckDuckGo and tools like ad blockers and tracker blockers to minimize online tracking.
- **Limit Personal Information Sharing:** Be cautious about sharing personal information on websites and with online services. Only provide necessary information when creating accounts or making purchases.
- **Email Encryption:** Use encrypted email services or tools to send sensitive information securely.
- **Device Privacy Settings:** Review and adjust privacy settings on your devices and apps to limit the data they collect and share.
- **Data Deletion:** Regularly delete or request the deletion of unnecessary personal data held by online services and social media platforms.
- **Privacy Policies:** Familiarize yourself with the privacy policies of websites and services you use to understand how your data is collected, used, and shared.
- **Educate Yourself:** Stay informed about evolving privacy threats and best practices for safeguarding your personal information online.]

Internet safety and privacy are ongoing efforts. By adopting these practices and staying vigilant, you can reduce the risks associated with online activities and protect your personal information from unauthorized access and misuse.

PASSWORD MANAGEMENT

MacBook password management involves creating strong, unique passwords for your user account and other accounts on the device, such as Wi-Fi networks and email accounts. It's essential to use strong passwords, avoid sharing them, enable two-factor authentication (2FA) when possible, and consider using a reputable password manager to securely store and autofill your passwords, enhancing the security of your MacBook and online accounts.

TWO-FACTOR AUTHENTICATION (2FA)

Two-factor authentication (2FA) is a security practice that adds an extra layer of protection to your online accounts. In addition to your password, 2FA requires you to provide a second verification method, typically something you have, such as a temporary code sent to your mobile device. This additional step makes it much harder for unauthorized users to access your accounts, enhancing online security.

6.

MACBOOK MAINTENANCE AND CARE

Maintaining and caring for your MacBook is essential to ensure its longevity and optimal performance. Here's a brief explanation of key MacBook maintenance and care practices:

Keep It Clean:
- Regularly clean the MacBook's screen, keyboard, and trackpad with a microfiber cloth to remove dust, smudges, and debris.

External Protection:
- Use a protective case or sleeve when carrying your MacBook to prevent scratches and dings.

Software Updates:
- Keep your macOS, apps, and drivers up to date by installing software updates and security patches promptly.

Backup Your Data:
- Regularly back up your data using Time Machine or cloud-based backup services to protect against data loss.

Storage Management:
- Maintain adequate free storage space on your MacBook to ensure it runs smoothly. Remove unnecessary files and applications.

Battery Health:
- Optimize battery health by avoiding extreme temperatures and keeping your MacBook's battery between 20% and 80% charged when possible.

Power Management:
- Adjust your MacBook's power settings to optimize performance and battery life according to your needs.

Protect Against Physical Damage:
- Avoid spills, drops, and physical damage by using your MacBook on a stable surface and keeping liquids away from it.

Security Measures:
- Enable security features like FileVault (disk encryption) and set a strong login password for data protection.

Malware Protection:
- Install reputable antivirus and antimalware software to protect against threats.

Wi-Fi and Network Safety:
- Connect to secure Wi-Fi networks and use a VPN for added privacy and security on public networks.

Screen Saver and Sleep Mode:
- Enable screen savers and sleep mode to conserve energy and protect the display.

Keyboard Covers:
- Consider using a keyboard cover to prevent dust and debris from entering the keyboard.

Regular Maintenance:
- Periodically clean the cooling system and vents to prevent overheating and improve airflow.

Customer Support:
Contact Apple Support or visit an Apple Store or Authorized Service Provider for hardware issues or repairs.
By following these maintenance and care practices, you can prolong the life of your MacBook and ensure it continues to operate at its best.

CLEANING AND MAINTENANCE

Cleaning and maintenance are essential for keeping your MacBook running smoothly and looking its best. Regular upkeep can extend its lifespan and ensure optimal performance. Here's an explanation of MacBook cleaning and maintenance:

Cleaning:
External Cleaning:
- Use a microfiber cloth to clean the MacBook's exterior, including the screen, body, and trackpad. Avoid using abrasive materials that could scratch the surface.
- If necessary, lightly dampen the cloth with water (or a mixture of water and isopropyl alcohol in equal parts) to remove stubborn stains or smudges.

Keyboard and Trackpad:
- Remove dust and debris from the keyboard and trackpad using compressed air or a soft brush.
- Consider using a silicone keyboard cover to prevent dust and spills from getting between the keys.

Screen Cleaning:
- Clean the screen using a microfiber cloth or a screen-cleaning solution designed for electronics. Gently wipe in a circular motion to avoid streaks.
- Avoid using harsh chemicals, abrasive materials, or excessive pressure on the screen.

Vent and Ports:
- Periodically use compressed air to clean the cooling vents and ports on the MacBook. This helps prevent overheating and ensures proper airflow.

Maintenance:
Software Updates:
- Keep your macOS, applications, and drivers up to date by regularly installing software updates and security patches.

Backup Your Data:
- Use Time Machine or cloud-based backup solutions to create regular backups of your data in case of hardware failure or data loss.

Storage Management:
- Maintain sufficient free storage space on your MacBook to prevent performance issues. Remove unnecessary files and applications.

Battery Health:
- Optimize battery health by avoiding extreme temperatures and keeping your MacBook's battery between 20% and 80% charged when possible.

Security Measures:

- Enable macOS security features like FileVault (disk encryption) and set a strong login password for data protection.

Malware Protection:
- Install reputable antivirus and antimalware software to protect against potential threats.

Wi-Fi and Network Safety:
- Connect to secure Wi-Fi networks and use a VPN for added privacy and security, especially on public networks.

Screen Saver and Sleep Mode:
- Enable screen savers and sleep mode settings to conserve energy and protect the display.

Regular Maintenance:
- Consider professional maintenance, such as cleaning the cooling system and vents, to prevent overheating and ensure proper airflow.

Customer Support:
- If you encounter hardware issues or need repairs, contact Apple Support, visit an Apple Store, or consult an Authorized Service Provider.

Regular cleaning and maintenance can help you keep your MacBook in excellent condition and avoid common problems associated with dust, debris, and software issues. It's essential to care for your MacBook to ensure it continues to perform at its best.

SOFTWARE MAINTENANCE

MacBook software maintenance involves various practices to ensure that the operating system and software applications on your MacBook run smoothly, securely, and efficiently. Proper software maintenance can help prevent issues, improve performance, and enhance the overall user experience. Here's an explanation of MacBook software maintenance:

Operating System Updates:
- Regularly update your macOS to the latest version available. Apple releases updates that include bug fixes, security patches, and performance improvements. Keeping your operating system up to date helps protect your MacBook from vulnerabilities and ensures compatibility with new software.

Application Updates:
- Keep all your installed applications, including web browsers, productivity software, and multimedia tools, up to date. Developers release updates to fix bugs and enhance functionality.

Security Software:
- Install reputable antivirus and antimalware software to protect your MacBook from malware and other security threats. Regularly update the security software's virus definitions and run scans as needed.

Backup Strategy:
- Implement a reliable backup strategy using Time Machine or cloud-based backup services. Regular backups safeguard your data against accidental deletion or hardware failure.

Disk Cleanup:
- Periodically review and clean up your MacBook's storage. Delete unnecessary files, applications, and old backups to free up space and improve performance.

Startup Items:
- Manage startup items to control which applications launch when your MacBook starts up. Limiting unnecessary startup items can lead to faster boot times.

Uninstall Unused Applications:
- Remove applications that you no longer use. Uninstalling unused software not only conserves storage space but also reduces potential security risks.

Privacy Settings:
- Review and adjust privacy settings for apps and services on your MacBook to control which ones have access to your personal information, location, and other data.

Clean Cache and Temporary Files:
- Clear cache and temporary files regularly to free up storage space and prevent performance degradation. You can use built-in macOS utilities or third-party tools for this purpose.

Browser Maintenance:
- Regularly clear browser caches, cookies, and history. Keeping your web browser optimized can lead to faster internet browsing.

Password Management:
- Use strong, unique passwords for your user account and online accounts. Consider using a password manager to generate and securely store passwords.

System Integrity Protection (SIP):
- macOS features System Integrity Protection to protect critical system files. Avoid disabling SIP unless you have a specific need and understand the implications.

User Accounts:
- Limit the number of user accounts on your MacBook and ensure that each account has strong, unique passwords. Restrict administrative privileges to minimize security risks.

System Preferences:
- Regularly review and adjust system preferences for power management, security, privacy, and network settings to suit your needs.

By following these software maintenance practices, you can keep your MacBook's software environment clean, secure, and up to date, ensuring that it operates efficiently and remains protected against security threats.

TROUBLESHOOTING HARDWARE ISSUES

Troubleshooting hardware issues involves the process of identifying, diagnosing, and resolving problems with the physical components of a device, such as a computer like a MacBook. Effective troubleshooting helps pinpoint the cause of hardware problems and, ideally, leads to their resolution. Here's an explanation of how to approach troubleshooting hardware issues:

Identify the Problem:
- Start by clearly defining and understanding the issue. Gather as much information as possible about the symptoms, error messages, and any recent changes or events that might be related.

Isolate the Issue:
- Determine whether the problem is specific to one component or if it affects multiple parts of the system. For example, is it a display issue, a keyboard issue, or something more widespread?

Check Connections and Cables:
- Verify that all cables, connectors, and peripherals (e.g., external monitors, hard drives) are properly connected. Loose or damaged cables can cause various hardware problems.

Restart Your Device:
- Sometimes, a simple restart can resolve hardware glitches or temporary issues. Try restarting your MacBook and see if the problem persists.

Check for Updates:

- Ensure that your operating system, drivers, and firmware are up to date. Manufacturers often release updates that include bug fixes and hardware improvements.

Run Built-In Diagnostics:
- Many devices, including MacBooks, come with built-in diagnostic tools. Use these tools to perform hardware tests to identify potential problems. On a MacBook, you can start by holding down the 'D' key during startup to access Apple Diagnostics.

Check for Overheating:
- Overheating can lead to hardware malfunctions. Make sure your MacBook is adequately ventilated, and the fans are functioning correctly. You can use temperature monitoring software to check for overheating issues.

External Devices and Peripherals:
- Disconnect all external devices and peripherals to see if the issue persists. Faulty external hardware can sometimes cause problems with your MacBook's performance.

Review Error Messages:
- Pay attention to any error messages or warning signs that your MacBook displays. These messages often provide valuable information about the underlying issue.

Backup Data:
- If you suspect a hardware issue that may require repairs, it's wise to back up your data to prevent potential data loss during troubleshooting or repair processes.

Consult Documentation:
- Read the user manual or documentation provided by the manufacturer to understand how your hardware components work and how to troubleshoot common issues.

Online Resources and Communities:
- Search online forums, manufacturer's support websites, and community resources for similar hardware issues and potential solutions. Others may have encountered and resolved similar problems.

Contact Manufacturer Support:
- If you're unable to resolve the issue on your own, contact the manufacturer's customer support or technical support. They can provide guidance, repair options, or warranty assistance.

Professional Repair:
- If all else fails and the issue is hardware-related, consider taking your MacBook to an authorized service provider or Apple Store for professional diagnostics and repair.

Remember that troubleshooting hardware issues can vary depending on the specific problem and device. It often involves a process of elimination, patience, and careful observation to identify and resolve the underlying cause.

7. ADVANCED MACBOOK USAGE

Advanced MacBook usage involves harnessing the full potential of your MacBook by exploring and utilizing its advanced features, settings, and capabilities. It goes beyond the basic functions and delves into more intricate tasks and customization options. Here's an explanation of advanced MacBook usage:

- **System Preferences Customization:** Advanced users often tweak their MacBook's settings through the System Preferences menu. This includes adjusting trackpad sensitivity, configuring keyboard shortcuts, customizing the desktop, and fine-tuning privacy and security settings.
- **Terminal and Command Line:** Advanced users may work with the Terminal application, which allows direct interaction with the macOS operating system using text commands. This is particularly useful for tasks like system maintenance, troubleshooting, and automation.
- **File Management:** Advanced users know how to efficiently manage files and folders. They can set up advanced file organization structures, use Terminal commands for file operations, and integrate third-party file management tools.
- **Multitasking and Productivity:** Advanced users make the most of macOS's multitasking features, such as Mission Control, Spaces, and Split View, to manage multiple applications and windows seamlessly. They may also employ keyboard shortcuts and third-party productivity apps.
- **Automation:** Automator and AppleScript are tools that advanced users leverage to automate repetitive tasks and create custom workflows. This can include automating file backups, batch-processing images, or managing email rules.
- **Security and Privacy:** Advanced users are proactive about their MacBook's security. They use features like FileVault for disk encryption, Firewall settings, Gatekeeper for app security, and regularly update software to protect against vulnerabilities.
- **Networking:** Understanding advanced networking settings and troubleshooting network issues is essential. Advanced users can configure VPNs, set up network shares, diagnose connection problems, and utilize advanced network tools.
- **Virtualization:** Some advanced users run virtual machines (VMs) on their MacBooks to run other operating systems or test software in different environments. Tools like Parallels Desktop or VirtualBox are commonly used for this purpose.
- **Coding and Development:** If you're a developer, you may use your MacBook for coding and software development. Advanced users might set up development environments, use version control systems (e.g., Git), and work with integrated development environments (IDEs).
- **Advanced Software:** Advanced users often employ complex software applications, such as video or audio editing software, 3D modeling tools, or scientific software, which require a deeper understanding of the software's capabilities.

- **Hardware Upgrades:** Some advanced users may be comfortable upgrading MacBook hardware components, such as RAM or storage, to improve performance. However, this can be a complex task and should be done with care.
- **Troubleshooting and Maintenance:** Advanced users have a solid understanding of macOS troubleshooting techniques. They can resolve software issues, deal with kernel panics, manage disk space effectively, and keep their MacBook running smoothly.

To become proficient in advanced MacBook usage, it's essential to continuously explore new features, stay updated on macOS releases, and, if necessary, seek out online tutorials, forums, and user communities to learn from experienced users. Remember that advanced usage may require more technical knowledge and carries a greater risk of unintended system changes, so always proceed with caution and back up your data regularly.

POWER USER TIPS

Power user tips are advanced techniques and strategies that experienced computer users employ to optimize their productivity, efficiency, and overall user experience. These tips often involve utilizing shortcuts, advanced settings, and lesser-known features of operating systems and software applications. Here's an explanation of power user tips:

- **Keyboard Shortcuts:** Power users rely heavily on keyboard shortcuts to perform tasks quickly without using a mouse. They memorize key combinations for common actions like copying, pasting, switching between applications, and opening specific functions within software.
- **Customization:** Power users take full advantage of customization options in their operating systems and applications. This includes personalizing keyboard shortcuts, tweaking interface settings, and customizing menus and toolbars to match their workflow.
- **Efficient File Management:** Power users are skilled at managing files and folders efficiently. They organize their files logically, use search functions effectively, and employ file naming conventions that make it easy to locate and manage documents.
- **Mastering Software:** They thoroughly learn and master software applications they use regularly. Whether it's office productivity suites, graphic design software, or programming IDEs, power users are proficient in utilizing advanced features and functions.
- **Automation:** Power users automate repetitive tasks using scripting languages, macros, or automation tools. This can involve creating scripts to process data, scheduling tasks, or automating complex workflows.
- **Multitasking Skills:** Efficiently managing multiple applications and tasks is a hallmark of power users. They leverage features like virtual desktops, window management tools, and task switching shortcuts to navigate between tasks seamlessly.

- **System Maintenance:** Power users are diligent about system maintenance. They regularly update software, manage startup items, clean up temporary files, and perform system optimizations to keep their computers running smoothly.
- **Security Awareness:** They prioritize cybersecurity by using strong, unique passwords, enabling two-factor authentication, and staying informed about security threats. Power users often use password managers and encryption tools to enhance security.
- **Advanced Searching:** They are adept at using advanced search operators to find specific information quickly. This skill is particularly valuable when dealing large datasets or extensive email archives.
- **Backup and Recovery:** Power users implement robust backup and recovery strategies to safeguard their data. This includes setting up automated backups, creating system images, and understanding data recovery options.
- **Resource Management:** They monitor system resources like CPU, RAM, and disk usage and can identify resource-intensive processes. This helps optimize system performance and troubleshoot issues.
- **Version Control:** For developers and collaborative projects, power users often use version control systems like Git to track changes, collaborate on code, and manage project versions effectively.
- **Troubleshooting**: When problems arise, power users are skilled troubleshooters. They can diagnose issues, interpret error messages, and find solutions independently or through online resources and communities.
- **Hardware Upgrades:** Some power users are comfortable upgrading hardware components like RAM, storage, or graphics cards to improve system performance or extend the lifespan of their devices.
- **Continuous Learning:** Power users are committed to staying up-to-date with technology trends, software updates, and new features. They invest time in learning new skills and tools to enhance their efficiency.

To become a power user, it's essential to invest time in learning and practicing these advanced techniques. This may involve reading user manuals, online tutorials, and participating in online communities and forums dedicated to your specific software or operating system. Power users often find that the increased efficiency and productivity they gain are well worth the effort.

VIRTUALIZATION AND DUAL BOOT

MacBook virtualization and dual boot are two advanced techniques that allow users to run multiple operating systems (OS) on a single MacBook computer. Here's an explanation of each:

MacBook Virtualization:
- **Definition:** MacBook virtualization is the process of running one or more guest operating systems concurrently on a host macOS system. This is achieved by using virtualization software that creates isolated virtual environments where the guest OS runs.
- **Virtualization Software:** There are several virtualization software options available for MacBooks, with some of the most popular being VMware Fusion, Parallels Desktop, and VirtualBox. These applications provide a platform to create, configure, and manage virtual machines (VMs).

Use Cases:
- **Compatibility Testing:** Virtualization allows you to test software or websites on different operating systems without needing separate physical machines.
- **Development Environments:** Developers can set up isolated development environments with various OS configurations to test and debug software.
- **Running Windows on Mac:** Many users use virtualization to run Windows applications on their MacBooks alongside macOS.
- **Security Testing:** Security professionals use VMs for safely analyzing potentially harmful files or software.

Advantages:
- **Resource Sharing:** Virtual machines can share resources with the host system, such as CPU, RAM, and storage.
- **Isolation:** VMs are isolated from each other and the host OS, which enhances security and stability.
- **Snapshot and Cloning:** You can create snapshots (backups) of VMs at specific points in time and clone VMs for different purposes.
- **Cost-Efficiency:** Running multiple OS instances on a single physical machine saves on hardware costs and space.

Considerations:
- **Resource Allocation:** You need to allocate sufficient resources (CPU cores, RAM) to each virtual machine for smooth performance.
- **License Requirements:** Some virtualization software and guest OS installations may require valid licenses.
- **Performance Impact:** Running multiple VMs simultaneously can impact the overall performance of your MacBook.

MacBook Dual Boot:
- **Definition:** Dual booting on a MacBook involves setting up the computer to run two different operating systems, typically macOS and another OS like Windows or Linux. When you start your MacBook, you can choose which OS to boot into.
- **Boot Camp:** Apple provides a utility called Boot Camp that simplifies the process of installing and managing a dual boot configuration on a MacBook. Boot Camp helps users create separate partitions on their hard drive for each OS.

Use Cases:
- **Running Windows Natively:** Dual booting allows you to run Windows as if it were on a PC, which can be advantageous for performance-intensive tasks or gaming.

- **Specific Software Requirements:** Some software may only run on Windows or other non-Mac operating systems.

Advantages:

- **Performance:** When running an OS natively, it can often perform better than in a virtualized environment.
- **Full Access:** Dual booting gives you complete access to the hardware resources of your MacBook for the selected OS.
- **No Virtualization Overhead:** There's no performance overhead from running virtualization software.

Considerations:

- **Storage Space:** Dual booting requires dedicating a portion of your hard drive to each OS, which can limit available storage.
- **Reboot Required:** You need to reboot your MacBook to switch between operating systems, which can be less convenient than virtualization.
- **Backup and Data Management:** Managing data across two separate OS installations can be more complex.

The choice between MacBook virtualization and dual boot depends on your specific needs. Virtualization is convenient for running multiple OS instances concurrently, while dual booting offers better performance when running a single OS natively. Consider factors such as the resources you have available, the software you need to run, and your preferences for ease of use when deciding which approach to take.

EXTERNAL DISPLAYS AND PERIPHERALS

MacBook external displays and peripherals are external devices that can be connected to your MacBook to extend its functionality and tailor your computing experience to your specific needs. Here's an explanation of MacBook external displays and peripherals:

External Displays:

- **Definition:** External displays, also known as monitors or screens, are additional visual output devices that you can connect to your MacBook. They provide extra screen real estate, allowing you to multitask, work with larger spreadsheets, edit videos, and more.
- **Connectivity:** To connect an external display to your MacBook, you typically use ports like HDMI, DisplayPort, Thunderbolt 3 (USB-C), or VGA, depending on your MacBook model and the monitor's compatibility.

Use Cases:

- **Extended Workspace:** External displays enable you to have an extended desktop, which is useful for tasks that require multiple windows or applications open simultaneously.
- **Graphics and Video Editing:** Graphic designers, video editors, and content creators often use external displays for better workspace organization and larger visual canvases.
- **Presentations:** You can connect your MacBook to projectors or large screens for presentations and meetings.

- **Gaming and Entertainment:** Gamers enjoy immersive gaming experiences on larger screens with high refresh rates, while users watch movies or stream content.
- **Resolution and Features:** External displays come in various resolutions (e.g., Full HD, 4K, 5K) and offer different features like touchscreens, HDR (High Dynamic Range), and various panel types (e.g., IPS, OLED).

Peripherals:
- **Definition:** Peripherals are external devices that you can connect to your MacBook to enhance its capabilities and tailor it to your needs. These devices include input peripherals (e.g., keyboards, mice, graphics tablets) and output peripherals (e.g., printers, scanners, external storage).
- **Connectivity:** Peripherals connect to your MacBook through various ports, including USB-A, USB-C, Thunderbolt 3, Bluetooth, and Wi-Fi, depending on the type of peripheral and MacBook model.

Common Peripherals and Use Cases:
- **Keyboards and Mice:** External keyboards and mice improve typing comfort and cursor control, making them essential for prolonged work sessions.
- **External Drives:** External hard drives and SSDs provide additional storage space, backup options, and data mobility.
- **Printers and Scanners:** These peripherals facilitate document printing, scanning, and digitization.
- **Audio Devices:** External speakers, headphones, and microphones enhance audio quality for entertainment and professional use.
- **Input Devices:** Graphics tablets, styluses, and MIDI controllers cater to digital artists, musicians, and creative professionals.
- **Docking Stations:** Docking stations consolidate multiple connections (e.g., displays, peripherals, Ethernet) into one hub for convenience and expandability.
- **Compatibility:** Ensure that your peripherals are compatible with your MacBook's operating system and port types. Some peripherals may require driver installations or firmware updates for seamless integration.
- **Wireless Peripherals:** Bluetooth-enabled peripherals eliminate the need for physical cables, providing greater flexibility and reducing workspace clutter.
- **Customization:** Many peripherals come with customizable buttons, macros, and settings, allowing you to tailor them to your specific needs and workflows.

In summary, MacBook external displays and peripherals are valuable tools for extending your MacBook's capabilities, whether you need additional screen space, extra storage, or specialized input/output options. When selecting external displays and peripherals, consider factors like compatibility, connectivity, use cases, and ergonomic considerations to create a versatile and efficient computing setup that suits your preferences.

 MACBOOK ACCESSORIES AND UPGRADES

MacBook accessories and upgrades are additional components and enhancements that can complement and improve the functionality of your MacBook laptop. These accessories and upgrades allow you to customize your MacBook experience, enhance productivity, and adapt to your specific needs. Here's an explanation of some common MacBook accessories and upgrades:

Accessories:

Laptop Stand:
- **Definition:** A laptop stand is an elevated platform that holds your MacBook at a comfortable viewing angle. It helps improve ergonomics by reducing strain on your neck and wrists.
- **Use Cases:** Better posture, improved cooling, and additional desk space.

External Keyboard and Mouse:
- **Definition:** External keyboards and mice can be connected to your MacBook for a more comfortable and efficient typing and navigation experience.
- **Use Cases:** Extended typing sessions, precise cursor control, and ergonomic benefits.

Laptop Bag or Sleeve:
- **Definition:** A laptop bag or sleeve provides protection and portability for your MacBook while on the go.
- **Use Cases:** Safe transport, organization, and style.

External Hard Drive or SSD:
- **Definition:** External storage devices expand your MacBook's storage capacity for backing up files, storing media, or running applications.
- **Use Cases:** Data backup, extra storage, and faster application access.

USB Hub or Docking Station:
- **Definition:** A USB hub or docking station adds extra USB ports and other connectivity options (e.g., HDMI, Ethernet) to your MacBook, increasing its versatility.
- **Use Cases:** Expanding connectivity, charging multiple devices, and connecting to external displays.

Headphones or Earphones:
- **Definition:** High-quality headphones or earphones provide better audio experiences, ideal for listening to music, watching videos, or participating in online meetings.
- **Use Cases:** Enhanced audio quality, noise isolation, and privacy.

Upgrades:
RAM (Memory) Upgrade:
- **Definition:** Increasing your MacBook's RAM can improve multitasking capabilities, allowing it to handle more applications simultaneously.
- **Use Cases:** Faster performance when running demanding applications or multiple tasks.

SSD (Solid-State Drive) Upgrade:
- **Definition:** Upgrading your MacBook's SSD can enhance overall system speed and responsiveness.
- **Use Cases:** Faster boot times, quicker application launches, and improved file access.

Battery Replacement:
- **Definition:** Replacing an aging MacBook battery can extend its battery life and usability.
- **Use Cases:** Longer use between charges and improved portability.

Graphics Card Upgrade (for select models):
- **Definition:** Some MacBook models support eGPU (external graphics processing unit) upgrades, which can significantly boost graphics performance for tasks like gaming or video editing.
- **Use Cases:** Enhanced graphics capabilities for resource-intensive applications and tasks.

Operating System Upgrade:
- **Definition:** Keeping your macOS up to date with the latest software updates and upgrades ensures you have access to new features, improved security, and better performance.
- **Use Cases:** Enhanced security, new features, and compatibility with the latest software.

Keyboard Replacement (for select models):
- **Definition:** In case of keyboard issues on certain MacBook models, replacing the keyboard can restore functionality and typing comfort.
- **Use Cases:** Improved keyboard performance and typing experience.

When considering MacBook accessories and upgrades, it's essential to choose items that align with your specific needs and budget. Not all accessories and upgrades are compatible with every MacBook model, so make sure to check compatibility before making a purchase. Properly chosen accessories and upgrades can significantly enhance your MacBook's usability and longevity.

RECOMMENDED ACCESSORIES

Recommended accessories for your MacBook can enhance your productivity, protect your device, and improve your overall computing experience. Here are some commonly recommended MacBook accessories, along with their explanations:

Laptop Stand:
- **Explanation:** A laptop stand elevates your MacBook to eye level, reducing neck and back strain. It promotes better ergonomics and allows for improved airflow, which helps keep your MacBook cool.
- **Use Cases:** Improved posture, enhanced cooling, and additional desk space.

External Keyboard and Mouse:
- **Explanation:** External keyboards and mice provide a more comfortable and efficient typing and navigation experience. They are especially useful for extended work sessions.
- **Use Cases:** Extended typing sessions, precise cursor control, and ergonomic benefits.

Laptop Bag or Sleeve:
- **Explanation:** A laptop bag or sleeve offers protection and portability for your MacBook while on the go. It helps safeguard your MacBook from scratches and minor impacts.
- **Use Cases:** Safe transport, organization, and style.

External Hard Drive or SSD:
- **Explanation:** External storage devices expand your MacBook's storage capacity for backing up files, storing media, or running applications. They are essential for data backup and extra storage.
- **Use Cases:** Data backup, extra storage, and faster application access.

USB Hub or Docking Station:
- **Explanation:** A USB hub or docking station adds extra USB ports and other connectivity options (e.g., HDMI, Ethernet) to your MacBook, increasing its versatility and convenience.
- **Use Cases:** Expanding connectivity, charging multiple devices, and connecting to external displays.

Headphones or Earphones:
- **Explanation:** High-quality headphones or earphones provide a better audio experience, ideal for listening to music, watching videos, or participating in online meetings. Noise-cancelling options offer added privacy and improved audio quality.
- **Use Cases:** Enhanced audio quality, noise isolation, and privacy.

Webcam Cover:
- **Explanation:** A webcam cover is a simple accessory that can be placed over your MacBook's built-in camera. It adds an extra layer of privacy by preventing unauthorized access to your camera.
- **Use Cases:** Privacy protection and peace of mind.

External Battery Pack (Power Bank):

- **Explanation:** An external battery pack can be a lifesaver when you need to charge your MacBook on the go. Look for a high-capacity power bank with USB-C Power Delivery support.
- **Use Cases:** Extended battery life when away from power outlets.

Screen Cleaning Kit:
- **Explanation:** A screen cleaning kit helps keep your MacBook's screen and keyboard clean and free of smudges, dust, and debris. It includes cleaning solutions, microfiber cloths, and brushes.
- **Use Cases:** Maintaining a clean and clear screen, hygiene, and longevity.

Thunderbolt 3 (USB-C) Adapters:
- **Explanation:** These adapters allow you to connect older USB-A, HDMI, VGA, or other devices to your MacBook's Thunderbolt 3 (USB-C) ports. They are particularly useful for compatibility with older peripherals.
- **Use Cases:** Connecting legacy devices and displays to your modern MacBook.

When choosing accessories for your MacBook, consider your specific needs and workflow. Make sure the accessories are compatible with your MacBook model and offer the features you require. Investing in the right accessories can greatly enhance your MacBook's usability and longevity while optimizing your overall computing experience.

UPGRADING MACBOOK COMPONENTS

Upgrading MacBook components involves replacing or enhancing internal hardware components to improve performance, expand storage capacity, or extend the life of your MacBook. However, it's important to note that not all MacBook models support user-upgradable components, and even on models that do, certain components may be challenging or impossible to upgrade. Here's an explanation of commonly upgradable MacBook components:

RAM (Memory) Upgrade:
- **Explanation:** Upgrading the RAM in your MacBook involves replacing or adding memory modules to increase the available system memory. More RAM can improve multitasking capabilities, allowing your MacBook to handle multiple applications more smoothly.
- **Use Cases:** Faster performance when running demanding applications or multitasking.

SSD (Solid-State Drive) Upgrade:
- **Explanation:** Upgrading the SSD in your MacBook can significantly boost overall system speed and responsiveness. SSDs are faster than traditional hard drives and provide quicker boot times, application launches, and file access.
- **Use Cases:** Improved system performance, faster data access, and additional storage capacity.

Battery Replacement:
- **Explanation:** Over time, MacBook batteries can degrade and lose capacity. Replacing the battery can extend your MacBook's battery life, ensuring longer usage between charges.
- **Use Cases:** Prolonged battery life, improved portability, and overall usability.

Graphics Card Upgrade (for select models):
- **Explanation**: Some MacBook models support eGPU (external graphics processing unit) upgrades, which can significantly enhance graphics performance for tasks like gaming or video editing. Internal GPU upgrades are generally not possible.
- **Use Cases**: Enhanced graphics capabilities for resource-intensive applications and tasks.

Wireless Card Upgrade (for select models):
- **Explanation:** Some MacBook models allow for wireless card upgrades to support newer Wi-Fi standards, providing faster and more reliable wireless connectivity.
- **Use Cases:** Improved Wi-Fi performance, compatibility with the latest wireless networks.

Keyboard Replacement (for select models):
- **Explanation:** On certain MacBook models with butterfly keyboards, keyboard replacement is possible if you experience keyboard issues or failures. The newer MacBook models have scissor-switch keyboards, which are more reliable.
- **Use Cases:** Improved keyboard performance and typing experience.

Operating System Upgrade:
- **Explanation:** Keeping your macOS up to date with the latest software updates and upgrades ensures you have access to new features, improved security, and better performance.
- **Use Cases:** Enhanced security, new features, and compatibility with the latest software.

It's essential to consider several factors when contemplating MacBook upgrades:
- **Compatibility:** Ensure that the components you plan to upgrade are compatible with your specific MacBook model. Apple often designs its laptops with non-user-upgradable components, so research your MacBook's specifications and limitations.
- **Warranty and AppleCare:** Upgrading certain components may void your MacBook's warranty or AppleCare coverage. Check your warranty status before making any upgrades.
- **Skill and Expertise**: Some upgrades, like replacing the SSD or battery, may require technical expertise and tools. If you're not comfortable with DIY upgrades, it's advisable to seek professional assistance.
- **Cost-Effectiveness:** Evaluate the cost of upgrading compared to the benefits gained. In some cases, it may be more cost-effective to invest in a newer MacBook model.

Before attempting any MacBook upgrades, it's wise to consult Apple's official support resources or seek advice from authorized service providers to ensure that the upgrade process is carried out correctly and safely.

UPGRADING RAM AND STORAGE

Upgrading the RAM (Random Access Memory) and storage on a MacBook can significantly enhance its performance and storage capacity, leading to a smoother and more responsive computing experience. Here's an explanation of upgrading RAM and storage in a MacBook:

MACBOOK GUIDE

Upgrading RAM (Memory):

Explanation: RAM is a type of computer memory that is used for running applications and temporarily storing data that is actively being used by the operating system and software. Upgrading RAM involves replacing or adding memory modules (RAM sticks) to increase the total amount of available memory in your MacBook.

Use Cases:
- **Improved Multitasking:** Upgrading RAM allows your MacBook to handle multiple applications and tasks simultaneously without slowing down. This is especially beneficial for tasks like video editing, graphic design, and running virtual machines.
- **Better Performance:** More RAM reduces the need for your MacBook to use slower storage (e.g., SSD) as virtual memory, leading to faster application launches and smoother overall performance.

Process:
- **Determine Compatibility:** Ensure that your MacBook model supports RAM upgrades and find out the maximum amount of RAM it can handle.
- **Purchase Compatible RAM:** Buy RAM modules that are compatible with your MacBook model and meet the specifications (e.g., DDR4, DDR3, or LPDDR4).
- **Installation:** Open your MacBook's case (varies by model), remove the existing RAM modules, and insert the new ones in the correct slots. Follow the manufacturer's guidelines for proper installation.
- **Restart:** After installing the new RAM, restart your MacBook, and it should recognize the increased memory automatically.

Upgrading Storage (SSD):
- **Explanation:** SSD (Solid-State Drive) is a type of storage that is significantly faster and more reliable than traditional hard drives. Upgrading storage involves replacing your MacBook's existing storage drive with a larger capacity SSD.
- **Use Cases:**

Increased Storage: Upgrading to a larger SSD provides more storage space for your files, applications, and media.
Faster Performance: SSDs offer faster data access speeds, resulting in quicker boot times, reduced application load times, and improved overall system responsiveness.

Process:
- **Back Up Data:** Before upgrading, back up your MacBook's data to an external drive or a cloud service to ensure you don't lose any important files.
- **Determine Compatibility:** Check if your MacBook model supports SSD upgrades and the type of SSD (SATA, NVMe) it requires.
- Purchase Compatible SSD: Buy an SSD that matches your MacBook's requirements in terms of form factor and interface.
- **Installation:** Open your MacBook's case (the process varies by model), remove the existing storage drive, and install the new SSD in its place. Depending on your MacBook model, this may require specialized tools or professional installation.
- **Data Migration:** After installing the new SSD, use a backup or migration tool to transfer your data from the backup to the new drive.

- **Operating System Installation:** You may need to reinstall macOS on the new SSD for a fresh start.

Upgrading RAM and storage on a MacBook can significantly extend the usable life of your device and provide a noticeable performance boost. However, the upgrade process can be complex, and it may void your warranty if not done correctly. If you're unsure about performing these upgrades yourself, consider consulting an authorized Apple service provider or a professional technician to ensure a successful and safe upgrade.

9. COMPATIBILITY AND LIMITATIONS

MacBook compatibility and limitations refer to the specific hardware and software constraints that you need to consider when using or upgrading a MacBook. These factors determine what you can do with your MacBook and the extent to which you can customize or enhance its capabilities.

Here's an explanation of MacBook compatibility and limitations:

Hardware Compatibility:
Operating System Compatibility:
- **Explanation:** The version of macOS (formerly OS X) that your MacBook can run depends on its hardware specifications. Newer macOS versions may not be compatible with older MacBook models.
- **Use Cases:** Ensuring that your MacBook can run the desired macOS version and access its features and security updates.

Processor Compatibility:
Explanation: Different MacBook models are equipped with various processors, which vary in terms of processing power and capabilities. Some software may require a certain level of processing power to run efficiently.
Use Cases: Understanding whether your MacBook's processor meets the requirements for running specific applications or performing resource-intensive tasks.

RAM and Storage Upgrades:
- **Explanation:** Not all MacBook models support user-upgradable RAM or storage. Some models have soldered RAM or non-upgradable SSDs.
- **Use Cases:** Determining whether you can upgrade your MacBook's memory and storage to meet your needs.

Port Compatibility:
- **Explanation:** Different MacBook models have different port configurations. For instance, some may have USB-C (Thunderbolt 3) ports, while others have USB-A, HDMI, and other ports.
- **Use Cases:** Ensuring that your peripherals, displays, and accessories are compatible with the ports on your MacBook.

Software Compatibility:
Application Compatibility:
- **Explanation:** Some applications may not be compatible with your MacBook's operating system or hardware. Developers may release software updates that require newer hardware or macOS versions.
- **Use Cases:** Checking whether the software you want to use is compatible with your MacBook to ensure it runs smoothly.

Security Updates:
Explanation: Older MacBook models may not receive security updates or support for the latest security features. This can leave your MacBook vulnerable to security threats.
Use Cases: Staying informed about your MacBook's update support cycle and considering upgrading to a newer model if security is a concern.

Upgrades and Repairs:
User-Upgradable Components:
- **Explanation:** Not all MacBook components are user-upgradable. Some models have limited upgrade options, such as non-upgradable RAM, soldered SSDs, or glued-in batteries.
- **Use Cases:** Understanding which components can be upgraded in your MacBook and planning upgrades accordingly.

Warranty Considerations:
- **Explanation:** Upgrading or repairing your MacBook on your own may void your warranty or AppleCare coverage. Apple may refuse service on a modified or damaged MacBook.
- **Use Cases:** Weighing the potential loss of warranty against the benefits of DIY upgrades and repairs.

Professional Service:
- **Explanation:** Some MacBook upgrades and repairs require professional service due to the complexity of the process or the need for specialized tools and expertise.
- **Use Cases:** Knowing when to seek professional assistance for upgrades, repairs, or troubleshooting.

Understanding MacBook compatibility and limitations is crucial for making informed decisions about using, upgrading, and maintaining your MacBook. Always consult official Apple documentation, support resources, and authorized service providers when in doubt about compatibility and upgrade options.

FUTURE OF MACBOOK

The future of MacBook, like other technology products, is influenced by emerging trends, innovations in hardware and software, and evolving user needs.

While I cannot predict specific developments beyond my last knowledge update in September 2021, I can provide some insights into the potential directions and trends that could shape the future of MacBook:

Performance Enhancements:

Expect continued improvements in processor performance, graphics capabilities, and RAM capacity. Apple's transition to its own ARM-based processors, such as the M1, may lead to even more powerful and energy-efficient MacBook models.

Form Factors and Design:

Apple has a history of pushing the boundaries of design and form factors. The future may bring thinner, lighter, and more compact MacBook models with innovative materials and build quality.

Display Technology:

Advancements in display technology may lead to MacBook screens with higher resolutions, increased color accuracy, and improved refresh rates. Mini-LED and micro-LED displays could become more prevalent.

Connectivity:

The adoption of faster connectivity options, including Thunderbolt 4, USB4, and improved Wi-Fi standards, will continue to enhance data transfer speeds and connectivity options for peripherals.

Battery Life:

Improved battery life remains a priority. Apple may leverage advancements in battery technology to offer even longer battery durations, further increasing the portability of MacBook devices.
Sustainability:

Apple has been emphasizing sustainability in its product design and manufacturing processes. The future of MacBook may involve more recyclable materials, energy efficiency, and efforts to reduce environmental impact.

Software Integration:
Tighter integration between macOS and iOS/iPadOS is likely to continue. Apple may introduce more cross-platform apps and features that seamlessly connect MacBook, iPhone, and iPad devices.

Augmented Reality (AR):
As AR technologies evolve, Apple may incorporate AR capabilities into MacBook models, possibly through enhanced webcams, sensors, or dedicated AR hardware.

Security and Privacy:
Expect ongoing improvements in security and privacy features to protect user data. Hardware-level security, such as the Secure Enclave, may continue to evolve.

Artificial Intelligence (AI):
AI-driven features and enhancements could become more prominent in macOS, optimizing performance, user experience, and personalization.

User Interface (UI) Changes:
Apple may introduce new UI design elements and interactions to enhance user experience and adapt to evolving user preferences.

Health and Wellness Features:
As technology plays a larger role in health and wellness, future MacBooks could include features like improved ergonomics, sleep tracking, and health-related sensors.

Modularity and Repairability:
There could be a shift towards more modular and repairable MacBook designs, addressing concerns about e-waste and offering greater flexibility for users.
It's important to note that Apple's product development is often shrouded in secrecy, and the company tends to unveil its innovations when they are ready for market. The future of MacBook will likely continue to be shaped by Apple's commitment to innovation, user feedback, and evolving technology trends. Keep an eye on official Apple announcements and product releases for the latest developments.

I-PHONE15 SENIORS

scan the qr code download for free
IPHONE 15 SENIORS GUIDE

MECBOOK GUIDE

Dear reader, if you're reading this sentence, you probably haven't carefully read the description of this book on the Amazon page, where the link to buy the COLOR version is clearly indicated at the end.
But don't worry, I have a surprise for you:
SCAN THE QR CODE TO DOWNLOAD AND ENJOY THE COLOR VERSION!

CONCLUSION

In conclusion, this MacBook guide provides a comprehensive overview of Apple's iconic laptop lineup, covering its history, hardware, software, and various aspects of its usage. We explored the evolution of MacBook models, delved into the essential hardware components, and discussed the capabilities of macOS, Apple's operating system.

Throughout this guide, we touched on compatibility considerations, provided insights into potential future developments, and offered recommendations for accessories and upgrades to maximize your MacBook's performance and utility.

It's important to remember that technology evolves rapidly, and the MacBook lineup continues to evolve with each new release. To stay current with the latest MacBook models, features, and announcements, we recommend regularly checking the official Apple website and reputable tech news sources.

We hope this guide has been informative and helpful in your journey with your MacBook. Whether you're a new user looking to get started or an experienced MacBook owner seeking to optimize your experience, we trust that the information provided here has been valuable to you. If you have any more questions or require further assistance in the future, don't hesitate to seek guidance. Thank you for using this MacBook guide, and we wish you a productive and enjoyable MacBook experience!

In the ever-evolving landscape of personal computing, the MacBook has remained a symbol of innovation and excellence. With each new iteration, Apple consistently raises the bar, pushing the boundaries of what a laptop can do. As technology advances, the MacBook lineup continues to adapt, offering users cutting-edge features, enhanced performance, and a seamless integration into the Apple ecosystem.

One of the MacBook's enduring strengths is its meticulous design. Apple's commitment to form and function has led to laptops that are not only aesthetically pleasing but also exceptionally functional. The unibody aluminum chassis, Retina displays, and industry-leading trackpads exemplify Apple's attention to detail and dedication to user experience.

Under the hood, the MacBook's hardware components are a testament to relentless innovation. The transition to Apple's custom ARM-based processors, exemplified by the M1 chip, signals a significant shift in the industry. These processors provide exceptional performance, power efficiency, and the foundation for an ecosystem of apps that can run seamlessly across Mac, iPad, and iPhone devices. This change promises a future where the MacBook continues to evolve and adapt to the ever-changing demands of modern computing.

The MacBook's software, macOS, has always been a key differentiator. Its intuitive interface, robust security features, and ecosystem integration have made it a favorite among creative professionals, developers, and everyday users alike. With each new macOS update, Apple introduces innovative features that enhance productivity, security, and convenience.

Looking ahead, the future of the MacBook appears bright. Anticipate further advancements in performance, display technology, and connectivity options. Apple's commitment to sustainability will likely lead to more eco-friendly materials and manufacturing processes, aligning with global environmental goals.

As the MacBook continues to evolve, it remains not just a tool for work and play but an essential part of our digital lives. It empowers creativity, fosters innovation, and connects people in ways that were once unimaginable.

In conclusion, the MacBook is more than just a laptop; it's a symbol of the relentless pursuit of excellence in technology. With its iconic design, powerful hardware, and intuitive software, it has earned its place as a trusted companion for users around the world. As we venture into the future, we can look forward to even more remarkable innovations from Apple, ensuring that the MacBook remains at the forefront of computing technology.

51411340R00063